HOW TO START A SUCCESSFUL AIRBNB BUSINESS

QUIT YOUR DAY JOB AND EARN FULL-TIME
INCOME ON AUTOPILOT WITH A PROFITABLE
AIRBNB BUSINESS EVEN IF YOU'RE AN
ABSOLUTE BEGINNER

WALTER GRANT

WITH
RICHARD ANDERSON

CONTENTS

Introduction   vii

PART ONE
THE FUNDAMENTALS

1. How does it work   3
2. How Safe Is Airbnb?   7
3. The Different Types of Airbnb   11
4. The Pro's and Con's of Being an Airbnb Host   17

PART TWO
THE PLANNING STAGE

5. Choosing a Business Structure   25
6. Conducting Airbnb Market Research   34
7. Market Research Tools   42

PART THREE
THE ACTUAL BUSINESS

8. Setting Up Your Airbnb Property   49
9. Cleaning and Resetting Your Airbnb Space   61
10. Creating House Rules   66
11. Creating a House Manual   73

PART FOUR
LET'S TALK MONEY

12. Understanding Your Airbnb Expenses   81
13. How Can I Make Money on Airbnb?   86
14. Pricing Strategies: Setting Your Price   92

PART FIVE
THE WINNING FORMULA

15. Avoid these Common Mistakes   103
16. Shooting Eye-Catching Photos   108
17. The Secrets to Creating the Perfect Listing Title   112
18. Crafting an Amazing Description That Sells
    Itself   115
19. Secrets to Increasing Your Search Rank   119
20. How to Get Five-Star Reviews   123

PART SIX
OPTIMIZING, AUTOMATING, AND SCALING YOUR BUSINESS

21. Automating Your Airbnb Business   129
22. Automating the Messaging   131
23. Automating the Cleaning   134
24. Automating the Pricing   138
25. Automating the Key Exchange   140
26. Automating the Entire Process   144
27. Scaling Your Airbnb Business   146

PART SEVEN
FAQS, ADDITIONAL TIPS AND A LIST OF TOOLS

28. Airbnb FAQs   153
29. Additional Tips   157

Conclusion   169
Resources   173

INTRODUCTION

Don't sit down and wait for the opportunities to come. Get up and make them.

MADAM C.J. WALKER

Megan used to live in a very nice part of Florida with her two beautiful kids. Though she had a lovely home, Megan had a major problem—her income as a teacher was not enough to pay her bills. However, quitting her job was not an option because her chances of getting a better one were slim.

Fortunately, Megan got to learn about Airbnb's short-term rental business. It was like a dream come true for her at the time. Megan and her kids made a habit of spending five weeks every summer at her mom's place, during which time her apartment was always empty. So, setting up the apartment for a short-term rental seemed like the perfect idea for

Megan to make extra cash. And guess what? In just five weeks, Megan was able to make a $2,000 profit on that single property! Sounds quite impressive, doesn't it?

Well, this book was designed to help you create a successful Airbnb story, just like Megan's, but better. The big question is "Who exactly is this book for?"

It is for:

• People like Megan, who are seeking alternative income sources because their current paycheck is not enough to settle their bills.

• Beginners in the Airbnb business who lack the confidence and practical knowledge needed to build a successful Airbnb business.

• Long-term landlords who want to divert their rentals towards hosting and short-term rentals.

• Experienced Airbnb hosts who have managed to survive through the introductory phase of their Airbnb businesses but are unable to maximize profit from their listings.

• People who aren't satisfied with their current job and are looking for a way out.

• People who would like to become their own boss, make decisions for themselves and not be managed by others.

• Anyone who wants to enjoy a life with more freedom and less constraint.

Can you relate to any of the above? Good, then this book is for you.

Starting a new business can be a daunting task, especially when it's your first time. But it is not as overwhelming if you have someone to guide you through the entire process from the beginning.

That is what this book is about. In each chapter, we break down everything you need to know about starting your own successful Airbnb business.

Some of the things you are going to learn include:

• A detailed walkthrough of the fundamentals of running an Airbnb business.

• The winning formula to hosting successful listings.

• Tips on how to offer your customers a remarkable experience and increase positive reviews.

• Tips for current landlords on how to transition from long-term rentals to short-term rentals.

• Tips on how to optimize your current listings, beat your competition to rank number one in the search results, and increase your profit margins.

• And much more.

One important thing to note about our stories is that being an entrepreneur is not always sunshine and rainbows. Your chances of success will largely depend on your efforts and commitment. As much as we don't want to sound discouraging in any way, we must emphasize that, while starting and maintaining Airbnb businesses can be fulfilling and fun, certain downsides and headaches come with Airbnb hosting. Fortunately, we have an entire section dedicated to helping you understand the best ways to deal with the most common and uncommon pitfalls in the Airbnb business.

Now, if you are here because you were unsuccessful in your first attempt at the Airbnb business, we need you to know that you don't have to feel guilty at all. This time, with the knowledge and guidance this book offers, success is a sure thing!

Every one of us certainly deserves to have a job we enjoy and that pays us well enough to live our best lives while still enjoying our work. Helping others create the best travel experiences they could ever get is certainly one of those jobs. And there is no better time to learn and acquire the resources, tools, and knowledge you need than now. So let's get started.

PART ONE
THE FUNDAMENTALS

CHAPTER 1
HOW DOES IT WORK

The successful online accommodation marketplace that you are about to get involved in was founded by Brian Chesky and Joe Gebbia. These folks were finding it hard to raise the rent for their San Francisco loft apartment, so they came up with the creative idea of placing an air mattress in their living room and turning the space into a kind of bed and breakfast. I guess we now know how the name "Airbnb" was invented—Air bed and breakfast. The roommates were able to earn $80 from each of their first three guests.

Though Brian and Joe originally came up with this idea just to make extra income, their initial success was quite impressive. Realizing how lucrative their idea was, Brian and Joe sought the assistance of another roommate, Nathan Blecharczyk, to help build the idea into a large-scale business. Finally, in 2008, these three co-founders used the concept to launch the multibillion-dollar online company that we see today.

Quite an inspiring story, isn't it?

————

How Does It Work for the Host?

Once you have a room, an apartment, or a property that you wish to place on a short-term rental, there are certain steps that you must take to fully register it as an Airbnb listing. For the newbies in the game, your Airbnb listings are the properties you register to be rented out to guests on the site.

The first thing to do before even registering your listings on Airbnb is to verify the laws and regulations concerning listing a rental in your city or neighborhood. Thereafter, you can go ahead and complete all the necessary paperwork and sign up properly on the Airbnb website. The registration process simply involves filling out basic information about yourself, uploading a profile picture, and attaching a verified ID that confirms the stated information.

Having created and verified your profile, the site gives you access to the section where you provide specific details about the space you are renting out. These details include the location of the space and the number of guests it can accommodate.

Next, you will add pictures of the space you want to list and fix your listing fees. The fees could be collected every night, week, or month. In the subsequent parts of this book, we will discuss further the best strategies to adopt to determine your property's market value and set a price to match it.

Now we know you want to ask: "How then are guests selected?" Guest approval in the Airbnb game is always up to you as a host. On the Airbnb site, you will find two features for selecting guests: the Instant Feature and the Request to Book Feature. When you choose the former, it simply means that your guests will be able to instantly book your space without waiting for any approval. However, when you choose the Request to Book Feature, you can size up your guests before accepting and approving their request to book your listing.

How Does It Work for the Guest?

The Airbnb website is designed in a way that makes it easy for guests to find and select the listings that best fit their dream destination. Before guests can browse the different listings available on the Airbnb site, they have to create a profile where they provide and fill out some basic information about themselves, including profile photo and ID. Just like with the hosts, guests' information will also be verified. They are also required to provide their requirements concerning travel and type of housing.

When guests find a listing they like, they can either book it immediately or request to book it, depending on the host's preselected preferences. In the case of a Request to Book, the approval has to be given within 24 hours of the guests submitting their requests. Once the request for the booking is approved, the guests then make payment and arrange the important details with the host, for example, how they will get the keys or passcodes to their accommodation or how to operate certain of the house's amenities.

CHAPTER 2
HOW SAFE IS AIRBNB?

This question worries both Airbnb hosts and guests. As a host, you think to yourself, "How safe is it to allow total strangers into my home?" In the same way, potential guests also think, "How safe is it to throw caution to the wind and live in a stranger's home?" As much as we may not want to believe it, there are real stories of how Airbnb guests and hosts were scammed, robbed, or assaulted. However, you shouldn't be discouraged; these incidents are rare. Most Airbnb hosts have never encountered any of these horrible incidents, so you don't have to worry! Here are a few recommended tips for the safety of both yourself and your guests:

- Get to know the other party very well

As experienced Airbnb hosts, we recommend that you don't go for the instant booking option, especially if you are a beginner in the short-term rental game. The instant booking option doesn't allow you to properly screen your guests before accepting their booking requests.

With the Request to Book option, you can get enough information about your guests to help you make better decisions. Firstly, you can start with their profiles. As a host or guest, you can easily check the profile of the other party to get to know them.

Apart from reading the details that your guests have provided on their profiles, you can also read the reviews left by your potential guests' previous hosts. This will give you an idea of the guests' behavior, how they treated the previous properties they stayed at, and if they are any red flags that you need to consider before approving their booking requests.

Aside from the profiles and reviews, interacting with your potential guests also allows you to screen them. The power of interaction between you and your guests cannot be overemphasized. This interaction helps to build a sort of personal connection between the two parties, which is a good thing.

- Hold all forms of communications within the Airbnb platform

Nowadays, it is quite tempting for Airbnb hosts to want to avoid the commission that Airbnb charges on each booking. In most cases, things don't turn out well for those who give in to such temptations. You must understand that Airbnb, being a secure online platform, enables you to communicate with your guests while ensuring the safety and protection of both parties.

As a host, you should never make any arrangement, especially in terms of payments, outside the Airbnb secure system. Once you do this, the company assurance policy is no longer valid. So if your valuables get stolen or damaged, you cannot be compensated. At the end of the day, you will realize that the security the Airbnb platform offers you is well worth the commission.

- Clearly state your house rules and expectations

One way you can protect yourself as an Airbnb host is to set out rules and expectations that your prospective guests will be obligated to follow. These rules could include prohibiting guests from staying out late at night, inviting other guests, bringing along pets, or smoking in your house. You should also mention which parts of your space are off-limits to guests. In addition to the house rules, you may include important safety directives that guests are expected to adhere to, like how and when they to use the different security systems, such as carbon monoxide detectors, smoke detectors, and so on.

As a host, you are expected to make your house rules as specific and as clear as possible. Also, before the booking is approved, there must be an agreement between you and your guests regarding the list of house rules.

- Install security systems, especially in off-limit areas

Even when you have clearly detailed your house rules, another problematic question that might arise for you as a host is, "How do you check if your guest is respecting your house rules whenever you are not there?" Introducing a little bit of technology by installing certain security systems, like security cameras, can help in this respect.

Although these home security systems have a lot of promising benefits, installing them can cause legal problems for you as a host. Using such a system could infringe on the privacy rights of your guests. The question is "How do we make use of these security systems while still adhering to Airbnb's legal terms and conditions?"

It is recommended that you don't install security systems right in the guest's space. Instead, you can install them in the off-limit areas where you have stored your valuables.

- Trust your instincts

In our experiences over the years as Airbnb hosts and entrepreneurs, one important lesson we have learned is that one's instincts are nature's way of giving one certain important signals. This might sound ridiculous. However, you must trust your intuition when dealing with guests. If you have dutifully carried out all the previously mentioned steps and you still don't feel comfortable with a particular arrangement, then just deny the request and find other guests.

CHAPTER 3
THE DIFFERENT TYPES OF AIRBNB

N ow that we have understood to a certain extent how Airbnb works as an online accommodation site for both the host and guests and how we can make it safe, let's address the different property types that can be registered as Airbnb listings. A fourteen-year-old student once asked: "Do all Airbnb spaces have to be on the Caribbean Islands?" Sounds funny, right?

Well, having a property on a Caribbean Island is a big plus. Nevertheless, Airbnb implements a higher level of flexibility in its accommodation options. As such, there is a wider range of listings that are accepted. There are standard housing options like bungalows, townhouses, guest suites, chalets, villas, cabins, apartments, cottages, hotels, hostel accommodations, and resorts. In the same way, the site allows you to rent out properties that can be considered "out of the box," like treehouses, safari tents, crypts, and tiny houses.

Even after choosing the property types you would like to register, you need to decide the specific kind of space you are interested in renting out. Airbnb spaces could be an entire property, a private room, or a shared room.

- Entire Property

Renting out an entire place means that your guests will have the freedom to use all parts of the property—that is, the living room, bathrooms, bedroom(s), kitchen, entrance, and yard. Most guests tend to pick this kind of space because they want privacy. Thus, the Airbnb properties in this category must have facilities that can be used exclusively by your guests.

Pros

As a host, renting out an entire property is extremely profitable. In just one night, you can earn four or five times what a person hosting a private or shared room will earn in a week.

Since the space is all theirs, your guests will be more comfortable during their stay. As such, there is a good chance that they would enjoy a better experience and leave positive reviews.

Cons

Since you are not there to supervise the guests' activities within your property, there is a higher risk of property damage.

Renting out an entire property demands a higher start-up

capital due to its high-priced purchasing/leasing cost. A lot of money also goes into its maintenance.

It also involves more cleaning than any other kind of space.

- Private Room

In the Airbnb business, a private room is a room in your home that you want to rent out to guests. You could have a private room with or without its own kitchen or bathroom. In cases where your guests will have to share these amenities, you have to indicate the number of people that are sharing them.

Pros

Private rooms are usually more affordable than renting out an entire apartment or house. Hence, a cheaper price is more likely to attract guests more rapidly and in larger numbers.

As an Airbnb host, less cleaning is required for private rooms.

Hosting guests in a private room in your own home gives you the chance to meet different people and experience different lifestyles without even traveling.

Cons

Though your cleaning work is reduced, it is still not as easy as renting out a shared room. Renting several private rooms at once may entail the same amount of cleaning that renting an entire property demands.

Not every guest or host is comfortable with the idea of socializing with others. So, things can get quite awkward when your guests find it hard to establish a friendly connection with you or the other guests.

- Shared Room

This option is the cheapest kind of space available on Airbnb. Its target market mostly comprises younger guests or travelers who are on a tight budget. A shared room is a living space with two or more beds that two or more guests will be expected to share during their stay.

Pros

A shared room is usually the best option for a new host with few financial resources. You will not have to spend much money on furnishing the space.

The budget-friendly price of a shared room gives you an advantage in increasing your potential guest list.

Guests who love meeting and connecting with new people are more likely to have a better experience in this kind of Airbnb.

Cons

Shared spaces tend to have sparse amenities, which could be a turn-off for guests.

It could dampen the enthusiasm of guests if they are not as extroverted as other guests.

- Airbnb Plus

Airbnb Plus comprises the finest quality homes that are selected based on their exceptional designs and the customer care services of their hosts. Airbnb Plus is a badge that has to be earned. To win it, your property must first be verified by Airbnb for unique quality, maintenance, and hospitality during an in-person inspection.

In most cases, properties that are selected in this category are furnished with everything that a guest would have in their own homes. For example, the kitchen would be equipped with a fridge, microwave, dishwasher, oven, and other cooking utensils; the bathroom may be supplied with high-quality shampoo and a hairdryer. The property could even come with exclusive outdoor facilities, like a swimming pool, gym, and so on.

Generally, only high-quality Airbnb spaces with superior designs and exceptional guest reviews earn an Airbnb Plus Badge.

- Airbnb Luxe

If you think that homes in Airbnb Plus are the most luxurious, then think again! As at the time of writing this book, Airbnb Luxe consists of 2,000 homes handpicked by experts from different parts of the world, including Bali, Lake Como, the Swiss Alps, St. Barts, Amalfi, and Santorini.

While Airbnb Plus is mostly about providing guests with a supreme accommodation experience, Airbnb Luxe consists of the world's most exceptional homes and locations. Each lodging experience comes with a trip designer. A trip designer is like a host who attends to your wishes 24/7. They also help you plan and organize everything from your airport transfers and restaurant reservations to your work schedule and excursions.

CHAPTER 4
THE PRO'S AND CON'S OF BEING AN AIRBNB HOST

There are certain advantages and disadvantages of running a short-term rental. Some of them are general and some of them are specific to being a host on Airbnb. Nevertheless, they are important to keep in mind when first jumping into this business.

What You Stand to Gain As an Airbnb Host

- Small- and large-scale source of income

The best motivating benefit is your earnings. Like the first two co-founders of Airbnb, Brian and Joe, many hosts start in the business because they want an extra source of income. However, in the long run, their success becomes so buoyant that hosting guests becomes a lifetime occupation for them.

- You get to meet people from interesting backgrounds

Being an Airbnb host helps you generate more than just money; you get to interact with people from different cultural backgrounds without you even visiting those parts of the world. You get to enjoy this benefit more when you are hosting in own your place because there would surely be more interaction between you and your guests.

While interacting with your guests, you might discover that most of them have interesting tales to tell. As such, by offering great customer service and a sympathetic ear, you will not only learn a lot but can also build long-lasting friendships. As an American host, wouldn't it be nice to have a friend from South Korea?

- It is convenient

Flexibility and convenience are two features that you enjoy as an Airbnb host. You are not obligated to host all the time, so you can choose what days, months, or seasons you want to host. For instance, in the introduction of this book, we spoke about Megan who only rented out her property for short-term rental during summer. You can choose to do the same.

Another way you get to enjoy convenience is Airbnb's built-in system for handling payments and bookings. Imagine if you had to do such jobs by yourself? It can be tiring, but being an Airbnb host helps you enjoy an easier rental process.

- You can screen your guests

One unique feature of the Airbnb review system is that it works both ways—your guests can write reviews based on their experiences in rented Airbnb spaces.

Similarly, you as a host can also read the reviews by previous hosts on the about your potential guests, their behavior as well as how they looked after their previously rented Airbnb space during their stay. This review system will encourage guests to be more careful and responsible with the amenities in your property during their stay.

- Your property is insured

Airbnb's Host Guarantee program offers Airbnb hosts up to $1 million as a kind of insurance against property damage by guests. Having such a safety net helps you, especially in unexpected situations where things go wrong. Nonetheless, it would be safer and wiser to secure your own insurance before setting up your Airbnb business.

But What About the Pitfalls of Being an Airbnb Host?

Everything good has a bad and ugly side. Running an Airbnb is no exception. As we emphasized in the introduction, being an Airbnb host can be extremely fun and fulfilling; however, there are certain downsides that you must prepare for in advance. Here are some of the pitfalls you will have to deal with as an Airbnb host:

- Erratic income

Unlike the stable income that is specific to the long-term rental business, your income as an Airbnb host will be erratic.

For instance, as a landlord who rents properties to long-term tenants, you can be sure of how much money you will earn at the end of each month or year, notwithstanding the state of the economy. However, when you are an Airbnb host, it is never easy to predict what your exact income will be at the end of every month because it tends to change from month-to-month.

To a large extent, bookings tend to be seasonal. There could be times where you could have a lot of bookings today and have a dry season tomorrow. Luckily for you, there are effective ways to combat dry seasons and be fully booked throughout the year. We will discuss this later in this book.

- Negative behaviors from guests

While being an Airbnb host offers you the chance to meet and interact with new people from different parts of the world, this cannot be achieved if your guests are not polite, responsible, and courteous. Occasionally, you will have to deal with nasty behavior from guests who will make their presence a nightmare for you. Thus, if you decide to start an Airbnb business, you must be mentally prepared to handle such guests effectively without ruining your brand image.

- Bad reviews

Customer reviews are an integral part of the Airbnb hosting system. Since your guests don't get the chance to tour the property ahead like in long-term rentals, these reviews serve as your only means of discovering the kind of experience they expect from your listings. As such, positive reviews will help attract more guests, while negative reviews will have the opposite effect.

Negative reviews can be a tough pill to swallow at the initial stage. There are cases where guests feel so entitled that they critique everything about the living spaces or property for completely unwarranted reasons.

No matter how much you try to avoid it, getting bad reviews is inevitable because you will always encounter unsatisfied and unhappy guests. Hence, if you decide to become an Airbnb host, you must learn to tolerate negative feedback without allowing it to negatively affect your morale.

Property damaged by guests

Another risk you must be prepared to handle when renting out to short-term guests is property damage. One in every three Airbnb hosts has had to deal with rowdy party-goers who trash amenities in the property when they come home drunk.

Although property damage is a risk, Airbnb's Host Guarantee program offers Airbnb hosts up to $1 million in compensation for property damage. There are, however, certain things that this compensation fee cannot cover, like damage to a rare artwork in your apartment or theft of something you cannot prove was there.

- Heavy workload

At this point, you might realize that running an Airbnb business involves more work than you had anticipated before reading this book. Many people tend to rush into starting their own Airbnb business because of the rewards it promises and the false idea of simplicity that most newbies often have.

So, you might think, "Okay. All I have to do is obtain a license and permission, create a profile, list my property on Airbnb for a profit, and then I can relax and collect the cash."

In the beginning, you will be more concerned with cutting costs and maximizing your resources. As such, you will find yourself doing a whole lot of cleaning, such as vacuuming the floor, dusting the furniture, and—what you might hate most —cleaning up the restroom and kitchen after each guest leaves.

Sometimes, you may have to deal with unexpected emergencies, like finding the toilet clogged a few hours before your guests are expected to arrive or helping them adjust the air conditioning. No matter what happens, you must ensure that everything is working well before your guests arrive. Unfortunately, these unexpected and inconvenient workloads are not a matter of "whether they will happen." Rather, they are a case of *"when* will they happen?" Like the other pitfalls we discussed earlier, you just have to deal with this workload.

PART TWO
THE PLANNING STAGE

CHAPTER 5
CHOOSING A BUSINESS STRUCTURE

W hether you have already acquired a rental property or not, you need to establish the type of business structure under which you are going to run your Airbnb business. So, what is a business structure? Why is it useful? What does it involve? Answering these questions and so many others will be our focus in the first section of your business's planning stage.

———

Choosing a Business Structure

A business structure is a type of organizational structure recognized by the law of the state or state in which your Airbnb operates. The business structure you choose for your Airbnb company will, to a large extent, influence everything about it, including its day-to-day operations, capital-raising opportunities, tax rates, and how much of your assets will be at risk if your business goes bankrupt. Your preferred business structure will also determine the kind of legal formalities you will go through to register your Airbnb business.

Each country has its unique set of business structures that its citizens can adopt. For example, in the U.S. there are four main types of business structures: sole proprietorship, partnership, limited liability company, and corporation. Each of these four business structures has its specific income, tax, and liability implications for both the Airbnb company and you as its owner. We will examine these four types of business structures.

- Sole Proprietorship

A sole proprietorship is the simplest organizational structure you can adopt for your Airbnb business. It is a one-man business structure, which means that you are the sole owner of the company. As such, you get to make business decisions whenever and however you want. You will also be responsible for your bookkeeping.

Although you have a trading name, you will still pay your taxes to the Internal Revenue Service in the form of self-employment taxes. The reason for this tax structure is that sole proprietorship companies are not regarded as separate business entities. In other words, the company's assets and liabilities are not considered to be distinct from its owner's assets and liabilities. So if your business goes bankrupt, you can be held personally liable for any debts or financial obligations you incur.

Pros

- A sole proprietorship is the easiest and simplest business structure to launch for different reasons, like low taxation and little paperwork.
- It involves less risk, which makes it the perfect option if you want to try out your business idea before starting a more formal business.
- You also enjoy complete control over your business.

Cons

- Raising money can be hard because banks are often reluctant to give loans to sole proprietorship businesses. You cannot sell stocks to potential shareholders either.
- Operating a sole proprietorship business structure will not protect you as an owner if your Airbnb business goes bankrupt.

- Partnership

A partnership is a business structure that can be adopted by Airbnb companies formed by two or more people. All the necessary conditions are usually documented in a partnership contract that is agreed upon and signed by the business partners. There are two common types of partnerships:

limited partnerships (LP) and limited liability partnerships (LLP). Each of these partnerships has distinctive features.

In the case of limited partnerships, only one general partner has unlimited liability, while the other partners have limited liability. Simply put, only one general partner can be held personally liable for the debts and financial obligations of the business, whereas the other partners will be protected in times of financial crisis. In most cases, though, this general partner is usually the person who binds the partnership.

Nonetheless, the general partner also has unlimited control over the company, while the partners with limited liability tend to have limited control. Like with sole proprietorship, partnerships are "pass-throughs," which means that their income "passes through" to their owners to be taxed as individual tax, and the general partner, who is the partner with unlimited liability, pays the same self-employment taxes as the other partners.

On the other hand, limited liability is a partnership in which some or all partners have limited liability. This type of partnership protects the personal properties and assets of all partners in cases of debt against the partnership business. So, no partner will be held responsible for the actions of another.

Pros

- In this type of business structure, all partners are in it together; so you and your colleagues can benefit from mutual support, knowledge, skills, experience, and contacts.

- Did I hear somebody say, "Two heads are better than one?" Exactly! The unique perspectives of each partner can contribute to better decision-making for the business.
- Unlike a sole proprietorship, it is easier to raise money because having more partners means having more money. Besides, your borrowing capacity from banks is likely to be greater than it would be if you opted for a sole proprietorship instead.

Cons

- In the case of a limited partnership, the general partner may find himself taking the fall for the actions of the other partners.
- Generally, each business partner, including the person who came up with the idea, will have to learn to compromise and demonstrate flexibility.

- Limited Liability Company

A limited liability company is a type of business structure that combines the features of two other business structures: the limited protection of a corporation and the simplicity and pass-through taxation that comes with running a sole proprietorship.

Too much to handle? Okay, let's break it down. Like we explained before, limited liability protects the business owner such that they will not be held personally liable in cases where a business gets into debt or faces legal sanctions.

By saying that LLCs, like sole proprietorship companies, offer simplicity and pass-through taxations, we mean that, by default, they are taxed just like a sole proprietorship; that is, the net income of LLCs passes through to the shareholders' individual tax return.

Think about it. Running your Airbnb business as an LLC means that you won't be taxed on individual and corporate levels as is typical of corporations. What is more, this business structure offers a bonus of limited liability protection, which sole proprietorship and limited partnership structures do not provide. Sounds quite profitable, right?

Pros

- As a beginner, registering your Airbnb business as an LLC is ideal, especially if you are starting small.
- Operating an LLC is a simple and cheap way to protect your assets, such as your houses, cars, and savings.
- It increases the credibility of your business, which could help you reach your target market and qualify for bank loans more easily.
- It also allows you to enjoy more tax benefits.

Cons

- Investors may be more interested in putting their money into a corporation, thus making it harder to raise financial capital as an LLC.

- Corporation (S-Corp and C-Corp)

A corporation is the most complex organizational structure that a business can adopt. When you adopt this structure, the liabilities and financial obligations of your business entity will be considered legally separate from the responsibilities of the business's owners and shareholders. As such, the Internal Revenue Service will tax the corporation at corporate tax rates and the corporation's shareholders at individual tax rates.

As a legal entity, a corporation has the right to draw up contracts, own assets, hire workers, and pay taxes. More importantly, it can also sue, and be sued by, other corporations.

Even if a corporation is sued, the law would offer limited liability protection to the corporation's shareholders. In other words, the shareholders cannot be held personally liable in cases of legal sanctions or bankruptcy.

Just like with the partnership structure, there are two common types of corporation structures: C-Corporations and S-Corporations. The major differences between these two subchapters are rooted mostly in their different tax rules and ownership.

C-Corporations have double taxation. With this type of corporation structure, the company pays corporate income tax and its shareholders are also made to pay federal income taxes through paid dividends. However, S-Corporations have pass-through taxation where shareholders report the company's income and losses on a personal tax return.

In terms of ownership, C-Corporations enjoy unlimited ownership. Anybody can be an owner, and there can be as many owners as you like. However, the ownership of S-Corporations is limited to a hundred shareholders—all of whom must be U.S. citizens.

S-Corps

Pros

- It is easy to raise financial capital.
- S-corporations are easier to manage than C-corporations because of the limited number of shareholders.
- Shareholders don't have to deal with double taxation.

Cons

- Though S-Corps incur low taxes, their taxes are more heavily scrutinized by the Internal Revenue Service.

C-Corps

Pros

- The corporation can have an unlimited number of owners. It also has unlimited funding opportunities.

Cons

- It is more complex to manage than an LLC.

Now that you know the different implications of each of these four business structures, it is important to carefully choose the type of business structure that you consider to be best for your Airbnb business. It will be more helpful to consult with your accountants, attorneys, or business counselors before making your decision, because you may decide to convert to another business structure someday and then face complications like tax consequences or even an unintended dissolution of your entire business.

CHAPTER 6
CONDUCTING AIRBNB MARKET RESEARCH

Once you have chosen your desired business structure, it will become easier to move on to the next stage of planning, which involves research. Generally, in real estate management, a great deal of thorough research is required before the acquisition of investment properties. In the same way, the secret to your success in the short-term rental business depends on your ability to collect and analyze relevant data with which you can make quick and informed decisions and actions before your competitors do so before you.

The only means of getting such relevant data is by conducting market research. Airbnb market research involves studying the unique regulations of your market, analyzing your target consumers and competitors, and so much more. You might be wondering, "What is all this hype about conducting market research for a job as easy as helping people live comfortably for a short time?"

The critical essence of conducting market research before building an Airbnb business cannot be overemphasized. Research offers you in-depth and verified data which can make it easier for you to acquire the best investment property. Even if you have already acquired your rental property, conducting quality research offers you leverage in your Airbnb business. The data you get from such research averts problems that could arise in the future. In short, the better your research, the better your understanding of your target market, and the higher your chances of ranking number one and outperforming your competition.

At this point, you will doubtlessly be convinced of the value of market research to the success of your Airbnb business. Therefore, let's get into the different ways to carry out market research in the planning stage of your Airbnb business.

- The Airbnb regulations in your city

In the first part of this book, we stated that your first task as a beginner is to verify the legality of running an Airbnb business in the city where you plan to acquire the Airbnb rental property. There are certain cities where it is illegal to rent out a property on a short-term basis. However, in cities where running an Airbnb is legal, there are usually laws that regulate the process of renting out homes or apartments for extended periods. Local regulations concerning short-term rental tend to differ from city to city.

Depending on your business structure, the legal requirements often demand that Airbnb hosts obtain certain permits or licenses to register their properties with the government or local council. All you have to do is approach the appropriate authority to learn what your city's regulations are governing Airbnb. Seek answers to questions like:

- Do you need a business license to list a property in your area?
- Are there certain rules that apply only to your area?
- Do you need a special permit to operate as an Airbnb host?
- Are there additional taxes you need to pay?
- Are there any requirements for the property?
- Does your area require an inspection?
- Are there any associations in your area that limit or forbid short-term rentals?

- Target market

Apart from the legalities of your Airbnb property, your target customers themselves are an important element that must be considered when planning your business. Of course, you want to attract enough guests to maximize profit from your listings. However, it is important to define the types of guests you want to target because not all categories of guests are your ideal guests.

Having an adequate understanding of your target Airbnb market makes it easier for you to build your property in a way that is appealing to such guests. And, eventually, you get to earn positive reviews and high ratings. How do you define your target market?

What type of guests do you want to attract? The first thing is to analyze your ideal demographic. Demographics information may include age, gender, age, income level, marital and family status, etc. Depending on your choice, your target market could be tourists, teenagers, businesspeople, older travelers, newly-wedded couples, families with kids, etc.

After identifying the kind of guests you want to attract, you also have to study those psychological characteristics that tend to influence the buying patterns of your target guests. We call these characteristics psychographics.

For instance, your target market may be young tourists. You may discover that these travelers are most likely to try out local dishes as they explore tourist attractions. With this information, you may focus on acquiring your Airbnb property in an area that has great local restaurants and unlimited access to nature and adventure.

If you have already acquired your property, conducting a target market analysis could also help decide how you can refurbish or design your Airbnb property so that it will better attract your target market. For instance, if you define your target market as high-income individuals and families, then you must upgrade your Airbnb space to one with luxurious and high-quality amenities and furnishings. In short, the insights you gain from identifying and studying your target guests inform and influence your overall marketing strategy, from your design and pricing system to your amenities.

- Neighborhood

Once you define your target guests and decide how you will attract them, the next step in your market research is to focus on finding a good neighborhood that will appeal to them. This mostly applies to Airbnb hosts who have not yet acquired their rental properties.

Why do you think people book Airbnb spaces? Well, many guests book Airbnb properties in order to attend business meetings and industry conferences or seek the most enjoyable ways to maximize their holiday experience. Generally, most Airbnb guests want to be near attractive and popular cultural centers or places such as beaches, restaurants, game parks, and city centers during their stay.

What does this tell us? The answer is simple. More than anything, the location of your Airbnb property plays an important role in determining if your business will be profitable or not. Fortunately, this significant element is something you can control during the planning stage of your Airbnb business. In your city, you will discover that every neighborhood has its potential investment locations. Some neighborhoods may appeal more to travelers and tourists than others. Which begs the question, "How do you assess the neighborhoods in your city to find the one that offers the best Airbnb investment opportunities?" Here are a few questions that can guide you in your research process:

- Where is the neighborhood located? Is the location appealing enough?
- Who are the people living in the neighborhood? Are they businesspeople, hipsters, or family-oriented folks?
- What unique attractions does the neighborhood offer? Does it have theme parks, clubs, nightlife, or beaches?
- Is the neighborhood a popular location in high demand?
- Are there many other Airbnbs in the location or are there just a few?

- Competition

Comparing yourself with your closest competitors is another important step to take when conducting Airbnb market research. However, you must understand that not every property close to yours might qualify as a competitor. For instance, if your Airbnb listing is a well-furnished two-bedroom apartment, then do not compare it to a four-bedroom bungalow with high-quality amenities. So how do you identify your competitors?

Firstly, they must be in the same neighborhood as your property or at least within range. They should also have the same spatial configuration as yours. Simply put, they must have the same number of bedrooms, bathrooms, kitchens, etc. They should also have similar finishes and amenities.

Once you have identified your competitors, analyze them using the following questions as a guide:

- What unique amenities are they offering? How do their amenities and furnishing compare to yours?
- How are these properties being priced on the Airbnb market? What does their calendar look like?
- What kind of reviews do they get? What is their overall rating?

You will surely gain a lot of insights from comparing yourself to your closest competitors. However, you need to resist the temptation to simply copy their strategies, which is what many new Airbnb hosts tend to do. Instead, use the information from your market research to improve and optimize your listings to become better and ultimately the best in the market. Imagine that you have already set a price that you think befits the kind of Airbnb space that you are offering. However, you then discover that the price is higher than that of your competitors who are offering a similar space with similar amenities. You can then take advantage of such information and set a better price that will not only attract your target market, but also help you maximize profits. Not to worry though—in the next two parts of this book, we will talk more about money and the best pricing tools for your Airbnb business, so stick with us!

- Trends

Being aware of trends in the Airbnb business is a smart move for both beginners and experienced hosts. When conducting your market research, you should also focus on collecting relevant data about current market trends, whether it's interior design trends or behavior trends, like utilizing eco-friendly objects in Airbnb spaces. You could also go the extra mile to study past trends because having such knowledge can help you better understand the kind of effects those trends have had on the Airbnb market.

- Occupancy Rate

Over the years, occupancy rates have become the ultimate metric for Airbnb hosts. As such, you must study the rate at which guests book Airbnb spaces in your area. Questions like the following can help your research:

Do occupancy rates rise and fall? If they do, then what is likely responsible for this fluctuation?

Are there any events that increase occupancy rates during a specific time of the year? For example, an apartment in New Orleans is likely to get more bookings than usual about a month before and during a well-attended event like the Mardi Gras.

With adequate knowledge of how occupancy rates work in your area, you can come up with strategies that will help you achieve high and optimized occupancy rates for most of every year.

CHAPTER 7
MARKET RESEARCH TOOLS

J udging from all that we have discussed so far, you will agree that Airbnb market research seems like a lot of work. But we have good news! Instead of doing all this work by yourself, there is a specific tool that you can take advantage of to make the process of data collection and analysis quite easy.

Tools to Use in Conducting Airbnb Market Research

- AirDNA

AirDNA is one of the leading companies today renowned for providing accurate and comprehensive short-term rental data and analytics from different parts of the world. It offers incredible value to Airbnb hosts using three separate tools: Market Minder, Investment Explorer, and Rentalizer.

- MarketMinder

Of AirDNA's three market research tools, MarketMinder is the most up-to-date tool. This state-of-the-art data-service tool allows you to search and discover new neighborhoods in your selected city for the best-performing short-term rental investments. It also helps you understand both historical and new trends by comparing the differences in their market performance.

MarketMinder can supply data on your competitors, which you can use to analyze their strengths and weaknesses as well as work out the best way to optimize the performance of your rental listings against theirs. With this tool, you can see how certain custom price strategies are created based on verified data using historical and future market demands.

- Investment Explorer

Investment Explorer was specifically designed to help Airbnb hosts discover short-term rental investment opportunities in the U.S. It supplies you with rental performance data from over 4,000 cities, as well as the amount of income that full-time Airbnbs are earning in each of these cities.

One unique feature of Investment Explorer is that it allows you to select one type of Airbnb space (for instance, a four-bedroom apartment) and get the rental Airbnb arbitrage that will be most profitable for that property. What this tool does is plot the average cost to rent against the average Airbnb revenue collected by the federal government of the United States.

- The Rentalizer

This AirDNA tool is also designed to help Airbnb hosts esti-
mate the profitability of a well-run Airbnb property in a
certain city or neighborhood. All you have to do is enter the
location and type of rental property, and Rentalizer will
supply you with a detailed report on the expected revenue
that you are likely to earn.

In addition, this tool has a feature whereby you can access the
revenue and occupancy rates of similar existing Airbnb properties at the address you provide. Unlike MarketMinder and
Investment Explorer which come at a hefty price, Rentalizer
is completely free to use for a certain time. However, like
Investment Explorer, it only operates within the U.S.

- Mashvisor

Mashvisor is another analytical and data service platform
that helps those interested in purchasing an Airbnb property
to determine if a property is a good investment or not. It
gives users an in-depth analysis of the property.

It also helps you find a profitable neighborhood in the city of
your choice. For example, Mashvisor's Airbnb Heatmap can
help you quickly perform a neighborhood analysis, using
filters like Airbnb Rental Income, Listing Price, Airbnb Cash
on Cash Return, and Airbnb Occupancy Rate.

One powerful feature of Mashvisor is that, when you want to
collect information, it pulls the desired data from different
trusted real estate and rental websites, like HomeAway,
Auction.com, etc. The data is then arranged in easy-to-read

and understandable reports that are suitable for even new Airbnb hosts. On the Mashvisor platform, data is pulled on a ten-month basis. However, it is updated once a month and the algorithm on the site is tested regularly to ascertain the accuracy of market trends and rental rates.

PART THREE
THE ACTUAL BUSINESS

CHAPTER 8
SETTING UP YOUR AIRBNB PROPERTY

N ow that we discussed the administrative side of the Airbnb planning game, it is time to move right into the practical aspect of preparing your Airbnb property for actual business.

Once you have conducted adequate Airbnb market research to get a rundown of what we discussed in the previous part of this book, the first question that is most likely to arise is, "How do I set up my Airbnb property in a way that will win the hearts of my guests?"

To answer this question, you must first understand that are a lot of differences between hotels and Airbnb spaces, aside from price. The most important is that when guests book into a hotel, they are undoubtedly aware that they are missing out on a lot of things. Hotels feel nothing like a home destination.

This disadvantage is what you as an Airbnb host are supposed to leverage when setting up your property.

A visually pleasing and well-stocked Airbnb property can feel just like a destination in its own right. It all depends on the efforts and commitment you put into setting up the different areas, including the bedrooms, bathrooms, kitchen, dining area, and living spaces. In this section, we will analyze the essentials for making each of these rooms unique, attractive, and comfortable.

Setting Up the Bedroom

As an Airbnb host, you must understand that a good night's sleep is one of the best ways to set the tone for your guests' successful stay. Hence, as you begin to set up the bedroom, your goal should be to ensure that your guests enjoy a comfortable night and start each day of their vacation feeling refreshed. Here are some of the basic bedroom essentials to consider during your set-up process:

- Comfortable beds and beddings

In an Airbnb bedroom, there is nothing more crucial than your guest having a comfortable foam mattress and a beautiful wooden bed frame. Don't assume that the bed is comfortable just by looking at it. Instead, hop into your guest's bed and sleep in it for a night to confirm that everything about it is perfect.

However, a comfortable bed is incomplete without clean sheets and pillows. To set up a standard bedroom, you are expected to provide a full set of high-quality, soft, and extremely clean sheets, including a fitted sheet, a top sheet, and pillowcases. A blanket, quilt, comforter or duvet is also necessary.

Just like your sheets, your pillows also have to be clean and soft. Most people sleep on two pillows, but you can go the extra mile and make it four, placing two on each side.

Even after providing all that we just mentioned, it is always best to tuck an extra set of bedding in the closet. Spills and accidents tend to happen, especially when your guests have kids. Though most guests may not make use of this bedding, the few who do will be pleased to know you left them emergency supplies.

- An area to unpack

When setting up your bedroom, you need to create a space where your guests can unpack. A simple wardrobe, shelf, closet, or dresser will do. But no matter the type of space you provide, it must be one in which your guests can unpack easily once they move in.

- Curtains

Apart from the bathroom, your guests also require complete privacy in their bedrooms. So, curtains are necessary when you set up the bedroom. Oftentimes, your guests may want to sleep in complete darkness and would rather not be disturbed by the sun rays in the morning. The curtains in the room can help in that respect. A decor tip that can be of help to you—you can create texture and depth in your Airbnb room by simply layering your darker curtains over delicate lace panels.

- Laundry baskets

Placing laundry baskets at designated spots in your Airbnb bedroom is another effective set-up strategy. By providing an intuitive space for your guests to properly dispose of dirty sheets and towels, you ensure that your guests keep the property clean, especially if they will be staying for a long time. Just in case you are confused about the best spot to place your laundry baskets, you can hide them under a bench or place them in a corner of the bedroom.

- Décor

Unlike what many people think, your bedroom also needs to be decorated, just like your living rooms. And a few aesthetic touches around the room could go a long way in making the room look more welcoming and unique. Your bedroom's décor plan could be as simple as hanging pictures of breathtaking landscapes, installing one or two flower vases, or even adding some nice colorful light bulbs. Just make sure that whatever you do makes the space feel more lively and happy!

Setting Up the Bathroom

More than the other parts of your Airbnb space, guests tend to notice when you intentionally invest time and effort in preparing the bathroom for them. Even if they don't end up cooking in your kitchen, or noticing the decorations in your living rooms, they will definitely appreciate the effort you put into cleaning and stocking the bathroom. Thus, setting up the bathroom is another chance for you to impress your potential guests and set yourself apart from your competitors. There are so many essentials you can offer to improve this simple space. Here are some of them:

- Appropriate shower fixtures

Though standard shower fixtures are quite affordable, it worthwhile upgrading your bathroom by fixing in an adjustable high-pressure showerhead and a shower hose. With such a feature, you can even charge a higher price while still ensuring that your guests enjoy a more comfortable shower experience.

Nevertheless, if you cannot upgrade your bathroom to include these items, then you must ensure that the available showerhead has enough water pressure; more importantly, it should have no limescale, which could spoil your guests' shower experiences.

- Hooks and shelves

Hooks and shelves are a must-have Airbnb for your bathroom. Hooks are essential for your guests to hang their clothes and towels. You could place the hooks at the back of the door or next to the shower to make it easier for guests to grab their towels after having a shower.

Now, as for shelves, your potential guests may come along with some of their personal items, like brushes, skincare products, etc. Installing shelves in the bathroom will make it easier for them to store those items.

- Toiletries and soap

Though some guests will bring their personal items for their stay, shampoo, hand soap, and body wash are still essential toiletries that you must place in your bathroom. The safest option for toiletries is one with neutral or no scent. This will help stop your Airbnb guests suffering allergic reactions to the fragrance or being uncomfortable with the scent.

- Clean set of towels

There is no question that towels are essential for every guest. The number of guests you accommodate in your property will determine the number of towels you will have to provide. If your Airbnb space offers access to facilities like pools, gyms, or spas, then you will also have to provide additional towels in the linen closet or shelves. This way, your guests will have enough towels to use after showering and during recreational activities.

All in all, you must ensure that the set of towels provided are very clean. An extra tip is for you to include in your Airbnb manual a place where guests are expected to store their used towels. You don't want to experience cases of moldy towels being hidden away in the bedroom cabinets for days or even weeks.

- Trash cans

Besides the laundry baskets that you place in the bedrooms, you can also place a trash can in each bathroom to make it more convenient for your guests to dispose of used toiletries after taking a shower or using the toilet.

You could also ask that they empty this trash can during their stay on the Airbnb property. This request should be clearly and explicitly stated in your house rules.

- Bathmats and foot towels

Bathmats and foot towels help to prevent slip accidents and protect your floors from excess moisture. With such anti-slip surfaces in the bathroom, your guests will be more at ease knowing they don't have to step directly onto wet floors after using the bathroom.

Using bathmats and foot towels also helps keep the floors clean. Still, you must ensure that they are always cleaned after every guest leaves. Regular cleaning will help prevent the buildup of mold and bacteria on the mats.

Setting Up the Kitchen and Dining Areas

If you are offering a kitchen and a dining space in your Airbnb listing, the best way to set them up is to imagine yourself cooking and eating different meals there. In this way, you can ensure that your Airbnb kitchen is equipped with all the kitchen essentials required for making different dishes. Here is a list of the necessities that should be stocked in your Airbnb kitchen and dining areas.

- Cookers and ovens

The basic function of the kitchen is to cook food, so it is only natural that you provide your guests with something to cook with. But first, you must understand that the type of cooking equipment you need will depend on your Airbnb listing price and target guests. For example, if you are charging a higher fee for your 'family-friendly' Airbnb property, then you will have to invest more money in your kitchenware. Along with a stovetop and oven, you could add in a decent-sized cooker and microwave that would suit a family.

- Pots and pans

Good-quality pots and pans are also necessary to provide your guests with an awesome cooking experience. Again, your target guests and Airbnb listing fees will determine if you need to provide a wide range of pots and pans or just a few of them.

- Fridge and freezer

Every kitchen needs a fridge and freezer. Hence, you need to provide a fridge whose size fits the size of the kitchen and the number of guests that you expect to host.

- Bowls and cooking utensils

These are quite important in your kitchen setup. Sometimes, your guests may want to bake or cook homemade meals that require the use of cooking bowls or utensils, like strainers, spatulas, serving spoons, wooden spoons, ladles, whisks, and tongs.

- Cutlery

Providing high-quality cutlery that will not rust or fade should also be a top priority as you set up your kitchen. You should provide enough to cater for the number of guests you plan to host. You could also add a few extra sets to prevent any shortages.

- Gloves and dishwashing liquid

If you don't want dirty dishes and pots stacked up in your kitchen after your guests leave, then you must ensure that you provide them with the necessary materials to clean up after they finish cooking and eating— this should include dishwashing liquid, some household cleaning gloves, towels and a dish drying rack.

Setting Up Living Spaces

Your living room is where your guests will most likely spend most of their day when they are not out exploring. As such, you must put a lot of effort into the décor and functionality of your living space. Let's get right into the elements you need to include in your Airbnb living area.

- Choose the right furniture

The kind of furniture you choose will play a great role in determining how appealing your guests will find your

Airbnb living area. So, how do you identify the right kind of furniture for your living space?

To start with, your furniture must adequately perform two important functions: Firstly, it must make the living area stylish and visually appealing. At the same time, it must also provide the kind of comfort that your guests need to enjoy their stay.

Nowadays, a lot of Airbnb hosts tend to get carried away in wanting to give their living space a unique vibe; thus, they end up choosing unusual furniture. Though this style could pass for good marketing, it can often backfire because guests who don't think the same way as their hosts might not appreciate the host's choice of furniture. The more distinctive your furniture style is, the greater the likelihood of this happening. So, what is the safest option, especially if you are a newbie host?

Your safest bet is to go for modern pieces of furniture that are more restrained but still stylish. This way, you are more likely to appeal to a wider range of guests.

- Avoid clusters in Your Seating Arrangement

While arranging your furniture in the living room, always ensure that you maximize the floor area. In other words, you are expected to provide ample seating space while still leaving enough free space in the room. Achieving such a balance requires you to be careful and creative. Moreover, being careful enough to choose the right kind of furniture can make your job a whole lot easier.

- Table area

What types of table will be best for your living space? Your choice of table will usually depend on the size of your living room. Circular tables may best suit your living area if you have limited space. They are space-efficient—that is, they offer you ample seating without using a large floor area. Nonetheless, square and rectangular tables are equally great, though they are better suited to Airbnb properties with larger floor areas.

It is also important that you consider the maximum number of guests your Airbnb can hold when deciding how much table area to provide in your living area. For example, if you have an apartment that can hold only four guests at a time, then you don't have to provide a large dining area that is better suited to a table of eight people.

- Provide entertainment and fast Wi-Fi service

It is quite true that nowadays your guests will most likely have their phones, laptops, iPads, and mobile data plans to stream videos and entertain themselves. However, nothing beats watching your favorite show or movie on a TV, while sitting comfortably on a couch in a visually appealing space, sipping from a glass of wine! Thus, as a host, you are expected to provide your guests with a smart television that offers interesting streaming options, like Netflix, Stan, and Amazon Prime.

Since you are offering a smart television with such streaming capability, then it is only right that you provide a fast Wi-Fi service so that your guests can enjoy what you have offered them. But you must ensure that the internet connectivity you choose is good enough to satisfy your guests as they stream and enjoy themselves.

EXTRA TIPS TO CONSIDER WHEN SETTING UP YOUR AIRBNB PROPERTY

- When choosing your furniture, stick to pieces of furniture that are finished with fabrics that are rated highly for safe washing.

- You could earn yourself some extra points by surprising your guests with food provisions in the kitchen.

- Provide items that guests usually forget to pack such as:

- A phone or laptop charger—it could be a spare Android smartphone, an iPhone, or a USB charger.
- A good physical map (because there are times when Google Maps can fail).
- Weather gears such as sunscreens and hats (for protection from harsh sun rays) or umbrellas and rain jackets (for when it rains).
- Reusable water bottles.
- Hairdryers.
- Earplugs.

CHAPTER 9
CLEANING AND RESETTING YOUR AIRBNB SPACE

As you begin the actual business of being an Airbnb host, the cleanliness of your Airbnb property must be your top priority. Failure to keep the space extremely clean tends to increase the chance of your guests complaining, leaving bad reviews, and even potentially asking for refunds. Good reviews are important for you to attract more guests and earn consistent revenue from your Airbnb listing. However, poor hygiene is a common cause of bad reviews. Fortunately for you, as a newbie host, you have more than enough guides to help you understand how the Airbnb cleaning process works.

As at the time of writing this book, the Airbnb platform stipulates a five-step cleaning process that all hosts are required to follow between each guest's stay. It could change in the future. Let's do a quick summary of this five-step cleaning protocol;

- Step 1: Prepare

Proper preparation entails ventilating your Airbnb space and using disinfectants that have been approved by your local regulatory agencies for use against COVID-19.

- Step 2: Clean

Cleaning involves sweeping, vacuuming, and mopping to remove dust and dirt from your Airbnb floors and counter-tops. It also includes washing dirty dishes and laundry at the highest possible setting.

- Step 3: Sanitize

Sanitizing entails the use of approved disinfectant spray to wipe spray high-touch surfaces such as doorknobs and TV remotes.

- Step 4: Check

In each room, refer to the best practices on each room-by-room checklist to make sure that all areas are cleaned and sanitized between each stay.

- Step 5: Reset

This step is aimed at preventing cross-contamination. Here, it is required that you safely dispose of or wash the cleaning supplies and protective gear used between each turnover. You are also advised to wash your hands before replacing guest supplies.

Apart from Airbnb's five-step cleaning process, you also have to check with your local city council to find out if it has any requirements for cleaning short-term rental properties. In some cities, the law demands that hosts follow a certain cleaning protocol in addition to the one set down by Airbnb.

Airbnb Cleaning Checklist for Each Turnover

Based on the five-step cleaning process stipulated by Airbnb, we have designed an effective Airbnb cleaning checklist that can help you maintain the cleanliness of your property while making your changeover as effective and fast as possible.

- Replace used towels, bedsheets, and linen with clean ones.
- Tidy and reset your bedroom and living room.
- Sweep and mop your floors.
- Vacuum your carpets or rugs.
- Clean and put away dirty dishes, cutlery, and cooking utensils.
- Empty the dishwasher and clean the fridge. Wipe any spills and pack out anything left behind by previous guests.
- Take out the trash.
- Wipe down all kitchen benches, countertops, tables, and other surfaces.
- Clean and polish the sinks, taps, and other hardware.
- Clean your toilets, bathtubs, and showers.
- Keep tabs on toiletries and supplies. Restock disposables when necessary.

- Check for damages to ensure that all gadgets, equipment, and appliances are working properly.

Airbnb Deep Cleaning Tips

Apart from the cleaning you do in between guest stays, you also have to engage in a deeper cleaning exercise at least once a month or once every two months. For many Airbnb hosts, deep cleaning an Airbnb space can be quite overwhelming, but it does not have to be the same for you. Here are a few tips you can use to effectively tackle each room within a short time:

- Always clear any visible clutters that are of no use at least a day before your deep-cleaning exercise.
- Ensure that you start deep-cleaning every room from the highest or hard-to-reach surfaces like the ceiling and baseboard.
- Save yourself the stress of taking down blinds or shades while deep cleaning your windows. Simply vacuum them using the brush attachment of the vacuum cleaner.
- To deep clean your floors more effectively, you could move all your furniture, even the large pieces, to another room.

Airbnb Cleaning Tips for Long-term Bookings

Guests who plan to spend more than a couple of days in a location might book your Airbnb property for 30-60 days.

Here are some tips you can use to ensure your property is clean during longer stays:

- Provide your guest with all the necessary cleaning products such as a vacuum cleaner, brooms, dustpans, garbage bags, cleaning buckets, cloths, etc.
- Perhaps, you could recommend a local cleaning service to your guests, if the standard and size of your Airbnb property is on a more luxurious level.

CHAPTER 10
CREATING HOUSE RULES

N o matter the kind of Airbnb space you are planning to rent out to guests, whether it's a small or large property, you need to have clearly stated house rules. Every Airbnb host needs to have them because the house rules for your Airbnb space are just as essential as the Airbnb listing itself. Explicit and written Airbnb house rules can serve as the perfect marketing tool to ensure that your home is booked by the right kind of guests. In most cases, it also helps prevent problems, especially in terms of guests damaging your property.

But first, what exactly do we mean by house rules in the Airbnb business? Airbnb house rules are professional codes of conduct where you, as the host, clearly state what your potential guests can and cannot do in your house and the penalties they risk incurring if they disobey any of these rules.

The legal responsibility of establishing the house rules falls to you as the host and rental owner. So you could decide the kind of style you want to use in writing them. It could be serious and formal or maybe fun and relaxed. Now I know all of this information can be quite overwhelming because you have never written Airbnb house rules before. Fortunately, we have prepared a step-by-step guide that can help you get started as you prepare to write your own house rules.

Before we go into that, you must understand that in writing your Airbnb house rules, you have to consider your target guests and their likely demands. Remember, you did your research on your target market during your planning stage. So you can use the relevant data you have previously gathered as a guide when writing your house rules too.

Now that we have gotten that out of the way, the next question is: "What things are you supposed to address when writing your house rules?"

- Check-In and Check-Out Times

One of the important things to include in your house rules is the stipulated times for checking in and out of the Airbnb property. We highly recommend that you state these hours very clearly if you want to avoid situations where one guest turns up for their booking way too early, only to find another guest on the property. Oftentimes, Airbnb hosts deal with cases of guests checking out later than expected. Such actions tend to disrupt the hosts' cleaning schedules. However, if you can clearly state the check-in and check-out times for your property and the likely consequences for anyone who fails to adhere to them (like payment of extra charges for overstaying), then you will probably avoid such problems.

- Property access

When you write your house rules, outline the areas of your property that are off-limits to your guests.

- Smoking

One mistake many new Airbnb hosts tend to make is that they assume their guests are aware that Airbnb operates a no-smoking policy. For this reason, they don't bother including the no-smoking rule in their official Airbnb house rules. But let's not forget that your guests are going to have nationalities and cultures that are quite different from yours, so it is in your best interest to emphasize in your house rules what your guest must do if they want to smoke on your property. It could include smoking outside and disposing of the cigarette butts in any of the trash cans provided.

Nonetheless, you could even decide to ban smoking completely on your rental property. At least, a total ban would save you from having to remove the cigarette odor from your home.

- Pets

Your house rules should also cover any restrictions regarding pets and pet sizes. Just like in the case of smoking, it is up to you as the host to decide if you want to allow pets in your Airbnb property or not. If you decide to make your property pet-friendly, you must consider the pros and cons of such a decision.

The positive side is that you are likely to attract more guests because nowadays more people are traveling with their pets. Also, having a pet-friendly space gives you the chance to charge a higher fee. However, here are some likely cons you should consider before opening your Airbnb property to guests with pets:

- Potential guests with pet allergies will not book your property.
- If your guests fail to look after their pets' needs, your place can become quite messy.
- Some parts of your property, especially your furniture and carpet, would be prone to extra damage.
- Hosting guests with pets means extra cleaning as some pets shed hair and leave lingering smells.
- Some pets, like dogs, can be pretty loud at night, which could disturb your neighbors.

- Eating areas

Another essential addition to your Airbnb house rules is to let your guests know the designated eating areas. It is more advisable to restrict the areas where your guests are allowed to eat or drink. Giving them full freedom to eat or drink wherever they want can increase the risk of them staining your sofa and bed covers with food.

Imagine your guests eating stir-fry spaghetti while under

your bed covers. It would mean more laundry for you. Thus, restricting the areas where your guests can enjoy their food is an effective strategy because it can save you hours at the laundry and money on stain removers.

- Unregistered visitors

As a newbie host, the no-unregistered-guests rule will help you cover a lot of bases. Then again, it could go both ways. In other words, you could decide to allow your guests to invite extra visitors to your property or you could enforce the rule that unregistered guests will not be allowed on your property at all.

However, even if you are comfortable with your guests bringing anyone along, it is better to limit the number of visitors, as such limitations can help protect your property from additional damage. If you enforce such a rule, your guests must agree in advance to pay extra fees if any visitors stay overnight.

- No parties

Remember what we said about the no-unregistered-guests rule covering a lot of bases for you as an Airbnb host? Well, this is one of those bases. To ensure that your guests do not turn your house into a nightclub, you must include a ban on parties in your list of house rules. Being very specific about the number of visitors goes a long way to enforcing this rule.

Generally, the party ban protects your property from the type of damage that usually occurs at parties when things spiral out of control.

- Noise and neighborhood

You cannot afford to have your guests disturbing the peace of your neighbors, especially at night. Your neighbors could destroy your Airbnb business with a simple call to your city council or even the police.

Hence, you must outline rules against making too much noise, especially late at night. Remember to be precise and clear when specifying in the house rules the hours your guests are required to keep noise to a minimum as well as the likely penalties they may face if they fail to adhere to this.

- Damage and compliance

Your Airbnb house rules will be incomplete if you don't attach penalties that your guests are likely to face if they violate your rules. Let your guests know what will happen to them if they disobey any rule.

Now, using the guide we have just analyzed, here is a sample that you can also use as a guide when drafting your own Airbnb house rules.

House Rules Sample

We kindly request that you read our house rules carefully and keep them in mind during your stay:

1. Please treat this apartment with the same respect as you would do your own home.

2. The maximum capacity of this property is four people, so no unregistered visitors or guests are allowed.

3. Do not eat or drink in the bedroom.

4. Smoking is not allowed inside the home, but you can smoke outside on the balcony. Also, please dispose of your cigarette butts in the trash can on the balcony.

5. Pets are allowed in the apartment but, please, do not allow them on the bed or sofa.

6. Parties and other kinds of events are not allowed in the apartment.

7. Our neighbors are important to us, and most of them live here full-time. So don't make any loud noise between 11 p.m. and 8 a.m.

8. Curfew begins at 11 p.m.

CHAPTER 11
CREATING A HOUSE MANUAL

Now we know you might be thinking, "Why are they repeating the same thing?" Well, your Airbnb house manual is not the same thing as your Airbnb house rules. They differ in terms of their content and purpose. We already know that your house rules are instructions that your guests are expected to adhere to so that everything can go smoothly during their stay.

On the other hand, the house manual is more like a guide that seeks to explain to your guests how they can find and use certain amenities and appliances, like the game station, Wi-Fi, coffee machine, and so on. It also contains other helpful information, like details of nearby attractions and events in the neighborhood that guests can attend to enjoy themselves.

Essentially, providing your guests with an explicit Airbnb house manual is like automating your Airbnb business. It contains answers to most of the questions that they are likely to have concerning different aspects of your property.

To create a successful house manual that will give you and your guests all the benefits we have mentioned above, you need to understand the exact information that goes into a house manual.

What essential piece of information should you include in an Airbnb House Manual?

- A brief welcome statement

Your Airbnb house manual should begin with a personal welcome message. A welcome statement helps you establish a connection with your potential guests, especially in situations where you will not be available to do an in-person check-in when they arrive. However, the message should be short!

- Your listing address and contact information

On the first page of your Airbnb house manual, you should include the address of your Airbnb property. It makes things easier for your guests when they need to call for a car service or order food.

The Airbnb manual should also include your contact information and your preferred means of communication—phone call, email, or text. The contact information comes in handy in situations where the content of the Airbnb manual is not enough to answer any questions your guests may have.

- Emergency contact and information

Sometimes, an Airbnb House manual can be a lifesaver in cases of emergencies. As such, you can dedicate a whole page on the Airbnb house manual to providing the contacts of emergency management agencies, like the police, fire department, and hospital.

Apart from these contacts, you should also provide adequate information on where to find fire extinguishers and how to safely exit the building during a fire outbreak, as well as other important emergency tips.

- Where to find appliances and amenities and how to use them

One of the advantages that Airbnb properties have over hotels is access to more appliances. But of what use will those appliances be if your guests cannot operate them? Your Airbnb house manual should provide clear instructions on how your guests can operate the appliances that they are allowed to use.

It should also explain the location of certain amenities. For example, you could mention that you provide makeup remover wipes for your female guests to use instead of towels and state where they can find these wipes.

- Local transport information

Transportation information is something your guests can research online. However, you can make things much easier for them by providing more information on subway stations or bus stops in the neighborhood. You could also offer them some insider tips on local transport in the neighborhood. However, you don't necessarily have to go into details.

- Sights to see and things to do

In the second part of this book, we discussed how you can research to gather relevant information about the unique and attractive places in your neighborhood. Well, this section is where you get to put all that research information to good use.

Your guests do not necessarily need you to provide a detailed guide of your area in your Airbnb house manual. They would rather appreciate it if you gave them an overview of what makes your area a unique and attractive destination.

You can get a bit more personal by recommending your favorite places to visit, your favorite things to do, and your favorite restaurants to eat at. Just in case you are confused about the kind of sights or events your potential guests might be interested in, here is a list that might be of help:

- Tourist attraction sites, like parks and museums
- Restaurants
- Shopping centers and grocery stores
- Fairs and festivals
- Attractive nightlife areas, like bars, clubs, playhouses, and music concerts

- Fun trip ideas, such as hiking or visiting a winery or hot spring

If possible, you could also include the websites, addresses, and photos of the places you recommend in your Airbnb Manual. This way, you also get to make the manual more engaging and visually appealing.

PART FOUR
LET'S TALK MONEY

CHAPTER 12
UNDERSTANDING YOUR AIRBNB EXPENSES

In the first three parts of this book, we focused on helping you understand the best strategies to use in making your Airbnb property "rental-ready," right from the fundamental stage to the actual business stage. So, what's next? We talk about money!

Your preparation, whether as a newbie or an experienced Airbnb host, would be incomplete without adequate knowledge of the financial side of the game. So, in this section, we will cover the operating costs you are likely to incur every year as an Airbnb host, the different profitable business opportunities in the Airbnb market, and, finally, the best pricing strategies and tools to use to automate your pricing process.

———

Understanding Your Airbnb Expenses

There are several costs associated with starting up and maintaining an Airbnb business. It is always wise to consider these likely expenses so that you can be more financially prepared. Here are some of them:

- Rent and security deposit

If you are interested in listing a rental property on Airbnb, you will have to pay a first-month rent and a variable security deposit to the landlord or property management company to secure the property. The actual amount paid as rent tends to vary from city to city and state to state. For example, renting apartments in Las Vegas may be cheaper than renting in cities like San Francisco.

An Airbnb host who rented some units in Mountain View, California, told us that the rent for each of those units tends to range from $1,800 to $2,800 a month. Also, he had to pay a variable security deposit of about $500. In some areas, landlords even ask for one month's worth of rent as a security deposit.

- Taxes

Once you rent out your home on Airbnb for more than 14 days, the IRS considers you to be a landlord, and so you will be required to report your rental income on your tax return. It is important for you to understand IRS's rules and to keep good and clean records in terms of payment of taxes.

- Insurance coverage

One immense benefit of running an Airbnb business is that your property is protected with a host guarantee of $1million. However, this is not all-inclusive insurance coverage. It does not cover most personal liabilities, like the theft of jewelry, money, pets, or rare artworks. Hence, it is advisable to get double coverage protection. To do so, you need to purchase commercial insurance coverage, like that of a bed-and-breakfast or a hotel.

- Furniture Costs

As a host, your furniture costs will depend on the type of property and the number of rooms you wish to rent out. Of course, it is cheaper to furnish a one-bedroom apartment than a two-bedroom apartment.

- Utilities and Subscriptions

In the typical long-term rental business, your tenant may be accountable for some or all of your in-house property's monthly utilities cost. However, in a short-term rental market like Airbnb, it is the host's responsibility to pay for all utilities.

Some of the utility costs you will likely pay as a start-up Airbnb business include water, electricity, internet, trash pickup, TV and streaming services, heating bills, and sometimes even parking fees. Owing to different factors, the costs of utilities tend to vary from month to month. For instance, due to the change of seasons, you may notice that your heating bills are much higher in winter than in summer.

- Costs of Soft Goods

Soft goods in this sense refers to the disposable items that you provide for your guests. Some of these soft goods include:

- Toiletries, trash, and storage bags.
- Shampoo, hand soap, and body wash.
- Laundry detergent, fabric softener, stain remover, etc., for cleaning.
- Salt, pepper, olive oil, etc., for cooking,
- Coffee, milk, tea bags, and sugar packets.

- Miscellaneous costs

As much as we have tried to give you a thorough update on all the costs you will likely face when you start out, we cannot predict everything. For example, there will be times when you may have to replace broken or spoilt amenities or pay to fix a malfunctioning appliance. During our first experience as Airbnb hosts, we had to spend about $100 to purchase blackout curtains for the two bedrooms in our Airbnb apartment. It was so unexpected. However, we did that because several guests had complained that the rooms were always too bright in the morning.

- Airbnb Service Fees

This expense is a constant one for every Airbnb host. Basically, for every reservation that is received, Airbnb charges a three percent service fee.

Essentially, you must understand three important facts about your Airbnb expenses:

Firstly, start-up costs tend to differ based on the type and size of your Airbnb property.

Secondly, as you become more experienced in the game, you will learn how to save money on certain expenses.

More importantly, you should not worry about maximizing profits, despite the many Airbnb start-up costs that we have just discussed. Airbnb in itself is a highly profitable business model. So, in the long run, your revenue will always exceed these expenses. Also, you do not get taxed on revenue but on profits alone.

CHAPTER 13
HOW CAN I MAKE MONEY ON AIRBNB?

Having clarified the expenses you are likely to encounter in the Airbnb game, let's discuss some of the most profitable business opportunities to earn more in the Airbnb market.

- Airbnb Investing

Investing in Airbnb rentals is an excellent strategy for real estate investors who want to earn maximum profits from multiple rental properties that they own. To be an Airbnb investor, you simply have to purchase rental properties, then list the entire property or individual rooms on the Airbnb platform for short-term rental, after following all the processes we discussed in the first three parts of this book. In most cases, Airbnb investors don't live in the properties that they rent to guests.

Pros

- The income you can earn from a well-run Airbnb far exceeds the income of running a long-term rental model.
- Investing in Airbnb gives you an inherent degree of flexibility in terms of pricing and the type of space you can offer.
- You will always have the choice of taking your properties off the Airbnb site and using them for other purposes if you so wish.

Cons

- Airbnb investing may not be the best option for you if you are interested in passive investment. This job involves your active presence, as there will always be the need for constant communication between you and your potential guests.

- Listing a rental property

Maximizing profits in the Airbnb rental market is not exclusive to investors or landlords who have the financial capability to purchase and own properties. To build a profitable Airbnb business, you could decide to start by listing a rental property.

In this case, you don't have to purchase or own any property, not even a room. All you have to do is rent a property—an apartment, condo, or bungalow—for the long term, and with the permission of your landlord, you could re-rent it to interested tourists and travelers on Airbnb.

To make a profit, you will need to set your rental Airbnb space at a price that will earn you an Airbnb revenue that will far exceed all your expenses, including the cost of renting the property itself.

Pros

- Since you are not buying the property, listing a rental property requires only a little upfront investment.
- Because it is not your property, you will not be responsible for paying the larger part of the expenses. So if, for example, the roof of the property were blown off in a storm, it would be your landlord's job to fix it and not yours.
- If a particular property doesn't seem to generate enough bookings to cover your costs, you can walk away and relocate to a more lucrative neighborhood.

Cons

- Whether you make enough income from bookings or not, you will always be obligated to pay your rent at the end of each month.
- Though you might not be held responsible for external damage, being the leaseholder, you will have to pay for repairs if your guests damage any amenities within the rented space.

- Listing an RV or Camper

Apartments, condominiums, and other short-stay homes are the type of rental properties that people commonly associate with the Airbnb rental market. However, you might be surprised to know that in many locations across the U.S., there are also quite a lot of RV owners who offer their campers on Airbnb.

There is quite a high demand in this market because many tourists and travelers would love to enjoy outdoor camping experiences without having to deal with the hassle of packing, driving, parking, and camping at different campsites. As an RV owner, you could cater to their needs and make adequate income from it.

Pros

- Renting your RV is an effective way to subsidize the cost of purchasing it.
- You can choose when you want to list your RV. It does not have to be all year round; instead, it could be during peak season, like summer or the holidays, or simply when you are not using it.

Cons

- If you don't own one, purchasing an RV can be quite expensive.
- If you are a full-time RVer, you will always have to deal with the hassle of removing every personal item

from your RV to prepare it for use by your guests.

- Renting out already-owned space

This business opportunity is particularly available for land-lords who may decide to change their property from being a long-term rental property to a short-term Airbnb rental.

Pros

- Short-term rental listings can help you earn more than what you earned as a long-term landlord.
- You get to enjoy more flexibility and convenience. You can select the specific days, months, or seasons you want to host.
- To an extent, your property is insured with the $1 million from Airbnb's Host Guarantee program.

Cons

- Your income will be erratic.
- Running an Airbnb business is quite different from being a long-term landlord. The former involves more work than you might have anticipated at first.

- Becoming a co-host or property manager

Over time, Airbnb has become so versatile that you do not have to purchase, own, or even list rental properties to earn an adequate income. Here is how it works: there are Airbnb hosts who have multiple listings but, for certain reasons, find it difficult to manage and monitor everything. Hence, they hire a third party to lighten their burden and help manage their properties. This third party is known as a property manager.

The original vacation rental owners add the manager to their listings using Airbnb's co-host feature. With this feature, the manager is recognized as a co-host. To boost their income, the property owner and the co-host share responsibility for various tasks associated with running the Airbnb business.

Pros

- As a property manager, you get to enjoy about 10-25 percent of the revenue earned from your listings without risking any investment in real estate.
- You can run more than one Airbnb at once.

Cons

- You could earn less than what the actual job is worth.

It is worth mentioning that Airbnb once had an automated payout system that paid automatically to both the host and co-host. This feature would have a notable benefit if it were still available.

CHAPTER 14
PRICING STRATEGIES: SETTING YOUR PRICE

Pricing strategies is an integral part of every Airbnb business. Your rental price must effectively define the maximum value of your Airbnb listing; in addition, it must be appealing enough to attract your target customers. An ideal price strategy does not undersell or oversell your listing. An underpriced rate lowers the value of your Airbnb listing, whereas an overpriced rate could make you lose potential guests.

Many newbie Airbnb hosts struggle to balance these two functions of price. And maybe they are not to blame because getting your Airbnb pricing strategy right the first time can be quite tricky. However, in the last section of this part, we have put together an effective guide that can help you nail your Airbnb pricing strategy on the very first attempt.

Types of Pricing Strategies

- Maximum Fill Rate Strategy

A maximum fill rate strategy is a pricing strategy that is most suitable if your business goal is to maximize your occupancy rate. So using this strategy, you will have to reduce your nightly price to attract more people. To make things clearer, your nightly price refers to the rate you decide to charge for your Airbnb space.

Nevertheless, using this strategy also requires you to play along with the pricing strategies of your competitors. However, because your aim is to maximize your occupancy rate, you would have to work to your maximum capacity to offer the best experience and more value than your competitors are offering.

- Maximum Rate Per Night Strategy

Using this price strategy, you will have to fix a high rate for nightly charges. Now the idea of profit here is that you can easily earn more and increase your net profit from individual bookings. Even if the number of bookings is reduced, your income will still be satisfactory. Unlike in the case of maximum fill rate, the goal with the maximum rate per night strategy is not to increase your occupancy rate, but rather to secure maximum profit with less effort.

- Long-Term Rentals Strategy

Using the long-term rental pricing strategy simply implies that you have to set your Airbnb pricing rates according to the typical long-term rentals (that is, monthly rates). If you want to adopt this pricing strategy, then you will have to draft out a rental agreement with your potential guests. You might even have to organize a house tour for your guests before they confirm the booking.

- Balanced Airbnb Pricing Strategy

Balanced Airbnb pricing strategy is the three-in-one pricing strategy. Adopting a balanced pricing strategy requires that you wisely integrate all three pricing strategies to efficiently and effectively manage your Airbnb business.

Using the balanced Airbnb pricing strategy in your business means that you will have a dynamic approach towards your Airbnb pricing. So, for example, you could easily shift between different types of pricing strategies to suit the season and demand in the Airbnb business. In high demand seasons, you could adopt a maximum full rate or maximum nightly charge pricing strategy to ensure maximum profit and increase your occupancy rate. However, in seasons with lower demand, you could go for the long-term rental strategy.

Questions to Ask before Framing Your Airbnb Pricing strategy

Even though we have examined the four different types of strategies you can adopt, you must answer some critical questions that can help you make the best choice for your Airbnb business.

- What type of Airbnb property am I renting out?

In the first part of this book, we analyzed the different types of properties you can list on Airbnb, from an entire property, like a bungalow or mansion, to a private area and shared rooms in your apartment. Well, it is important that you consider the type of Airbnb property you are listing before and when framing your pricing strategy. You must ensure that your rental price aligns appropriately with the type of property you are renting. For instance, if you are renting out an entire luxurious property, you could easily go for a maximum night rate pricing strategy. Such a strategy could work because your property would offer more to your potential guests so they are likely to pay more.

- What amenities am I offering?

Your guests pay you in exchange for the services that you provide in your Airbnb space. Thus, you should also consider the kind of amenities you intend to offer your potential guests. If you are offering few amenities, then it would be unwise to demand a high rental. However, if your property is packed with numerous luxurious amenities, like a swimming pool, a gym, or even a spa, then you will most likely attract more customers and profits, even if you charge high rates.

- Who are my target guests?

There is no way you can decide on your pricing strategy without considering your potential guests. If your target audience is young and adventurous backpackers, then, surely, using the maximum night rate strategy would be a bad choice for business. However, this type of strategy could help increase the number of bookings and profits if your target audience comprises tourists and travelers on family vacations.

- Who are my competitors?

Every Airbnb guest tends to consider and compare the prices and reviews of different competitors before booking their choice. As such, your potential guest can also be your competitor's potential guest. This is why your competitors are quite important when deciding which pricing strategy to adopt.

Firstly, you should consider the number of competitors in your neighborhood. If you find yourself operating in an overly competitive area, then either the maximum fill rate strategy or balanced Airbnb pricing strategy may be the best option to compete in this market. However, if you have only a few competitors, you can without doubt achieve more profits using the maximum night rate strategy.

Aside from looking at the number of competitors you have, this is where you should use your Airbnb market research, specifically the data on competitive analysis. This way, you can study not only your competitors' pricing strategies but also their strengths and weaknesses. Having gotten adequate information regarding your competitors, you can adopt a strategy that will differentiate you from your competitors so that guests will book your property rather than theirs.

- What are my financial and business goals?

Your business and financial goals, whether they are monthly or annual goals, play a crucial role in choosing an Airbnb pricing strategy. You will notice that each of the four types of pricing strategies has a specific set of goals. Thus, identifying and considering your business goals will make it even easier for you to choose an effective pricing strategy.

Here are a few examples to show the connection between your business goals and your choice of Airbnb pricing strategy: if your annual goal is to increase your occupancy rate, then the maximum fill rate strategy would be a good option because setting your nightly charges below average would surely attract more guests. On the other hand, a maximum night rate or balanced Airbnb pricing could be more beneficial if your annual business goal is not the numbers but the profits.

Automating the Process of Pricing with the Best Pricing Tools

From what we have discussed so far, it is quite clear that, as an Airbnb host, you can easily maximize your income potential if you always change your rental rates to hit the sweet spot where demand meets availability. However, keeping track by yourself can be unreliable because of the volatile nature of the rental market—prices can fall or rise at any time. As such, you may end up finding yourself one step behind every time.

However, with smart and dynamic pricing tools, you can automate the pricing process and get better predictions for the most suitable prices of property rentals.

A dynamic and smart pricing tool helps you to constantly monitor market activity and then uses real-time, hyperlocal data to automatically adjust your rates so that you get booked at the best price and time. So, if your competitors lower their rates on a particular date, your chosen dynamic pricing tool will also lower your rates accordingly. However, in cases where there is increased demand and more availability in the Airbnb market, perhaps because of a popular event in your area, the dynamic pricing tool will automatically increase your rates to leverage the increased demand.

To get all these benefits, you just have to integrate your Airbnb site with a dynamic pricing tool. Here are three of the best dynamic pricing tools you can consider integrating with your Airbnb listing:

- PriceLabs

This smart pricing tool is an innovative revenue management tool for Airbnb hosts to automate their pricing system. As a data-driven tool, it helps you manage rental prices and stay restrictions which, in turn, increases your Airbnb revenue and saves you hours of research.

Pros

- The cost of integrating PriceLabs with a listing tends to reduce as you continue to use it for more listings.

- This smart pricing tool can be used in any location, even in places with little market data.
- It is quite easy to use and less dependent on market data.

Cons

- Its load time is a bit long. Sometimes you may have to wait up to thirty seconds for the calendar to load.
- It is quite expensive for hosts with low occupancy rates.

- Beyond

Beyond is another effective revenue management tool with great features when it comes to solutions that provide dynamic pricing and maximize revenue growth. To determine accurate daily rates, Beyond analyzes over a billion data points daily while taking several variables into account, such as seasonality, day of the week, and local events that could affect the market demand for your market. All prices offered by the tool tend to fluctuate around the base price you set.

Pros

- The algorithm this tool creates a competitive daily rate that covers up to twelve months into the future.
- It is less expensive than PriceLabs.

Cons

- You might need to monitor their pricing. It's not something you set up and forget, especially in between on and off-seasons.

- Wheelhouse

A team of PhD data scientists and revenue management veterans also built an efficient revenue management tool that analyzes over 10 billion data points every night to optimize your pricing based on real-time market demand. The pricing recommendations from Wheelhouse vary depending on historical booking performance, real-time market activity, seasonal trends, and local demand.

Pros

- This smart tool updates your rental rates every night to enable you to make more income in high seasons and get more bookings more in low seasons.
- Wheelhouse charges cheaper commissions on your booking revenues.

Cons

- The charges are not flat per unit, which means you won't pay for the product, but for its services. Thus, any incremental revenue could mean an additional commission for you.

PART FIVE
THE WINNING FORMULA

CHAPTER 15
AVOID THESE COMMON MISTAKES

G one are those days when being an Airbnb host simply involved setting up a rental listing, exchanging emails with potential guests, and charging them to stay in your home for a short period. Nowadays, the Airbnb market has become so competitive that you cannot afford to be mediocre. It is almost like embarking on a new career path. Well, it is, actually!

To be able to stand out and build a profitable Airbnb business, you need to understand the most effective Airbnb strategies. In this part of the book, we will reveal the winning formula which comprises all the strategies you need to become a Superhost. But first, you must identify the problems that prevent many Airbnb hosts from getting the results they were expecting.

———

Avoid these Common Mistakes

Firstly, understanding the most common Airbnb mistakes helps you identify what mistakes you have to look out for or what mistakes you are currently making as an experienced host. When you acknowledge all these potential pitfalls, you will find it easier to understand the best winning strategies that are most appropriate for your situation. So what are these common Airbnb mistakes?

- Uploading bad pictures

One of the easiest ways to create a bad first impression on your guests is to upload photos of your Airbnb listings that were shot in poor lighting and from bad angles. Unfortunately, this mistake is quite common, especially for new Airbnb hosts.

What many don't know is that photos are one of the most important factors that guests consider when booking a listing. So how do you expect to entice your guests enough to book your listing when the quality of your photos suggests that you lazily shot them while standing in your doorway?

Avoid taking bad pictures so that you do not lose a large segment of your potential client base. Instead, strive to take stunning photos of your Airbnb listing. Luckily for you, we have an entire section in this section where we will discuss how you can take the best pictures of your Airbnb listing. So stick with us!

- Providing incomplete listing information

The idea of starting up your own Airbnb business can be so overwhelming that you may feel tempted to rush your listing process. Truly, we understand your eagerness to get it over with so that you can start booking guests and making your own money. However, such a decision could cost you a lot in the end.

While choosing an Airbnb, your guests need to have a complete picture so they can visualize what kind of experience your space can offer. Thus, the title, description, and every other necessary information about your listing must be carefully and efficiently drafted.

- Not communicating effectively with your guests

In the Airbnb business, the importance of effective communication between you and your guests cannot be overemphasized. Thus, it would be a big mistake if you did not acknowledge this fact.

From the very moment your potential guests contact you to the point when they leave a review after their vacation, the way you handle every step of the communication process matters. The amount of time it takes you to respond, how you respond, and the completeness of your responses can have a great impact on both your guests' experiences and your listing rankings

As an Airbnb host, avoid the first basic communication error —don't take too long to respond to your potential guests' requests, both before and after they check in. Instead, show them that they are in safe hands and that you care about their experiences by responding quickly to any requests. Remain consistent when communicating with them. Keep in touch when they check in, during their stay, and after they check out.

- Failure to clean your property thoroughly

The cleanliness of your Airbnb listing is the first thing your guests are likely to notice when they arrive. It is also one of the major factors that will determine if your guests leave positive or negative reviews. Thus, failing to maintain the cleanliness of your home is a costly mistake that you must avoid, as it could destroy your business, especially when the business is in its infancy.

Poor reviews in the Airbnb market are mostly the result of uncleanliness. Such negative reviews strongly dissuade potential guests from booking your listing before you even get the chance to interact with them. How do you avoid this particular mistake? Keep every area of your Airbnb listing—especially the bedrooms, bathrooms, and kitchens—spotless.

- No dynamic Pricing Strategy

In the previous part, we explained how your pricing strategy is an integral part of your Airbnb business. The biggest pricing mistake you can make is to use a single price for an entire year. Making such a decision could cost you a whole lot of money, especially during spikes in demand.

To prevent this error, take advantage of the dynamic pricing strategy. By using this scheme, you will become more responsive and more competitive. And, as we said in the previous chapter, you could always automate the prices by using smart pricing tools, like Wheelhouse and Beyond.

Now that we have successfully identified the common mistakes, let's go straight into the different strategies that make up the winning formula.

CHAPTER 16
SHOOTING EYE-CATCHING PHOTOS

As experienced hosts, we can confidently say that the photos of your Airbnb space are what initially attracts your potential guests whenever they browse through your listings. Every photo you upload is a powerful tool that could either make or break your chances of winning them over.

When your Airbnb photos display your rental space and all that it offers at its finest, then your listing will likely get lots of views and even appear among the top listings in search results. The good news is that producing eye-catching photos is not as hard as you think; you do not even have to be a professional photographer. The task only requires the right amount of planning and effort. Here are some helpful tips to take superb pictures that will attract your potential guests and upscale your rental listing.

- Declutter, clean and stage your Airbnb space

The first step to taking eye-catching photos is to adequately prepare every room and stage the space in the best possible way. You must ensure that every part of your Airbnb rental is spotless and pristine. Nothing puts off guests faster than pictures of a disorganized and dirty property. Here is a summary of what the preparation processes should include;

- Pack away any clutter that could make your Airbnb space look smaller than it is.
- The furniture in your living rooms and bedrooms must be arranged well.
- The bathtub, shower, and sink must be thoroughly cleaned. You can give your bathroom a more luxurious feel by placing some candles and folded towels in it.
- Wash and pack away dirty dishes. Your countertops must be sparkling clean, while your cooking utensils must be neatly arranged.
- Your floors must also be vacuumed and mopped so that they sparkle.

- Generate great lighting

Having prepped your room properly for the photoshoot, the next important element you need to shoot eye-catching photos is great lighting! Not only does great lighting make your Airbnb photos look more professional, but it also helps in enhancing the contrast, depth, and colors of the photos.

Before you begin taking interior photos of your listing, turn on all the lights and open the doors, curtains, and maybe windows where appropriate. Turning on all indoor lights helps eliminate any dark corners from your photos. It also creates an inviting atmosphere.

However, once you begin to take the shots, you should avoid aiming straight at the opened windows, especially when the sunlight is very bright. Your camera lenses will not be able to handle the contrast between bright windows and a dark room.

- Always shoot corners

Common mistakes that some photographers tend to make is stepping far into the room to snap, or shooting straight at a wall. However, shooting a corner gives more dimension to the composition of your photos. For example, in your bedroom, shooting a corner would mostly involve you using your bed as the focal point to make the room look larger and more inviting. To give a better perspective to the entire space, it is best to use the same rule for every other room in your property.

- Take photos from different angles

As you shoot, don't take every photo from the same angle. Rather, make an effort to add some variety by taking the shots from different angles. A fair warning though—ensure that you are not carried away as you try to be more artistic with your photos because capturing all the amenities the guests want to see is what matters the most.

- Paint a unique personality using the details in your Airbnb photos

Every major and minor detail of your Airbnb space must communicate the unique personality that it can offer your guests. Guests tend to appreciate it when the photos of a listing they are considering booking are more practical. For instance, if your property offers a rustic lifestyle, then your pictures should have detailed shots of amenities like a copper tea kettle and a cheeseboard.

CHAPTER 17
THE SECRETS TO CREATING THE PERFECT LISTING TITLE

Having taken eye-catching photos of your Airbnb space, the next winning strategy is to write a catchy title that perfectly describes what those photos are trying to communicate. Just like your Airbnb photos, the description title helps to draw the attention of your potential guests. It is like a teaser that gives your potential guests a glimpse of what your property is offering. Here are a few tips to consider when creating the perfect listing title:

- Address the specific needs of your audience

Addressing the needs and expectations of your potential guests can help you come up with the best title for your Airbnb listing. For instance, if you are offering your Airbnb space specifically to newly-wedded couples who want to enjoy a memorable vacation or honeymoon, then your title must include something that appeals to the needs of such guests. You could include something like this in your title: A Newly Renovated Luxury Home with a Secluded Beach, Perfect for a Romantic Getaway.

- Capture the best features of your property

Your property's best features should be the major highlight of your listing title. By showcasing these features, you will capture your guests' attention. It answers the basic questions of every guest, one of which is, "What does this property have to offer me?"

- Avoid using generic words in your title.

Two out of every listing title you find on Airbnb will include words like "beautiful," "comfy," and "convenient." Avoid using those words at all costs because they describe just about every Airbnb space. The best thing to do is use unique and illustrative adjectives that best portray the character of your property and help you stand out; some of which could include:

- Rustic
- Eco-friendly
- Contemporary
- Eclectic
- Secluded
- Insta-worthy
- Hideaway

- Efficiently utilize your Character Limit

The Airbnb platform allows you only fifty characters to write a catchy title that will help promote your Airbnb space. For this reason, every word you include must create a real impact on your guests' booking choice.

If this word limit makes it difficult for you to paint the best picture with your words, you could try using abbreviations and symbols. These will make it easier for you to add more details to your title while still making it short, sweet, and simple. Here are a few common Airbnb abbreviations (and a symbol) that could be of help to you:

- BA, to mean *bathroom*
- APT, to mean *apartment*
- BR, to mean *bedroom*
- AC, to mean *air conditioning*
- Using a heart symbol to replace the word "love"

CHAPTER 18
CRAFTING AN AMAZING DESCRIPTION THAT SELLS ITSELF

The same kind of effort that you put into capturing top-quality Airbnb photos and writing your listing should also be used in crafting your listing description. Though your Airbnb photos and listing titles are the first things that capture the interest of your potential guests, your listing description is that marketing tool that fixes their interest. It provides more important information to encourage your guests to book your space.

Now, do you have to hire a professional copywriter to craft an amazing description for your listings? Not necessarily. There is an art to writing an enticing description that will sell your listing. Let's find out the steps that make up this art.

- Acknowledge the needs of your target audience

Since your listing title has addressed the specific needs of your potential guests, your description should analyze and elaborate on how your Airbnb space can satisfy the needs and preferences of your target audience. So if, for instance, your listing title mentions that your property offers a romantic getaway, you could break down the kinds of amenities or features the property has that qualify it to deliver such offers.

- Provide details that answer questions your potential guests might have

As you write your descriptions, remember that you are trying to help your target audience to visualize your space as clearly as possible. Hence, you must walk them through every detail. Give them an idea of what each room offers.

Aside from the rooms, you should also include details about the amenities that are available both inside and outside your Airbnb space. Examples of amenities that guests are usually interested in include toiletries, extra towels, hairdryers, cooking items, utensils, etc. You could also include outdoor amenities, like a gym, pool, BBQ area, etc. All these details help your potential guests in their decision-making process.

- Elaborate on the best features of your space

Besides including all general details about your Airbnb space, you also have to elaborate on the property's unique selling points highlighted in the listing title. So a part of your description should answer questions like: "What makes your space stand out from others?" and "What is great about your location or the amenities within the property?" Thus, you could mention something about the house being near a very popular tourist site or there being a Jacuzzi.

- Call to action

Try to make your description stand out from others by a closing statement or two that will direct your potential guests to choose you. Though it is not quite commonly used, it can make a whole lot of difference in encouraging your potential guests. A call to action could be written like this;

I'm looking forward to hosting amazing guests like you. I will be waiting to get an inquiry from you so that we can start discussing more details.

- Structure your description well enough

No one, not even the most enthusiastic guests, would want to read a description that looks like a long essay. Thus, it is highly recommended that you structure your listing description into a series of paragraphs, with each paragraph containing the following:

- A brief introduction.
- A room-by-room description,
- A general description of the outdoor spaces and location.
- A description of your unique selling proposition
- A call to action.

With such a clearly defined structure, your guest can easily find and digest the information available. Overall, you should keep your listing description brief but not generic.

CHAPTER 19
SECRETS TO INCREASING YOUR SEARCH RANK

Optimizing your listing by using Airbnb SEO is another component of the Airbnb winning formula. Now let's break it down. SEO stands for Search Engine Optimization. When we speak of Airbnb SEO, it involves strategies that can help improve your search rankings on Airbnb.

Increasing your search rank means that your Airbnb listing becomes one of the top listings that appear on the first page of Airbnb-related search results. Being a top listing will increase your chances of getting more bookings.

The secret to increasing your search ranking lies in your ability to understand how the search algorithm actually works and the factors that influence it. Here are some factors that you can leverage to increase your search ranking.

- Update your calendar

Most guests are interested in learning about your calendar availability and verifying the listing information and rates you provide. So, if you update your Airbnb calendar regularly, the Airbnb algorithm tags you as an active host. This identity, in turn, increases your chances of having a higher search ranking. To make the job of updating calendars even more convenient for you, you can use a project management software application, like Smartbnb, which helps automatically update your calendar.

- Use the Instant Book feature

Remember, in the first part of this book, we explained that the Airbnb site has two options with which guests can book depending on the choice of the hosts? Most guests tend to prefer booking quickly and with no obstacles. As such, listings that enable the Instant Book feature tend to occupy the first few pages of Airbnb-related search results.

So, for you as a host, enabling the Instant Book feature can be an impactful way to increase your search ranking. If you are not completely comfortable with the idea of allowing any guests in your home, you could limit access only to guests with secured IDs

- Get more five-star reviews

Good reviews are quite important for attracting more guests. However, gaining as many five-star reviews as possible will surely have a more powerful influence on your search ranking. The Airbnb search algorithm takes into account the number of guests you have hosted and the reviews and ratings left by these guests. If you have many five-star reviews (which of course means higher ratings), the search algorithm will increase your search ranking and place your Airbnb listings as one of the top listings. But how exactly do you gain more five-star reviews? Well, that question tackles another part of the winning formula that we will get to discuss soon.

- Promote your Airbnb account on social media

Moving beyond the Airbnb site and promoting your Airbnb listing on other platforms is an effective strategy that can make an immense difference in your search ranking. Fortunately, creating a social media presence for your Airbnb listings is quite easy.

Once you have successfully set up your listing on the Airbnb site, you can share it on your Facebook, Instagram, Twitter, or LinkedIn pages. You can also ask your friends, colleagues, and loved ones to share it on their own social media pages too. With such an effective strategy, Airbnb will surely and immediately boost your search ranking.

- Set competitive prices

Price is also one of the biggest factors that guests consider when trying to book an Airbnb. Knowing this, the search algorithm pushes and promotes affordable listings or listings that offer special pricing offers, like custom promotions or length-of-stay discounts.

Hence, to increase your search ranking, especially as a new Airbnb host with no reviews and ratings, you could adopt the maximum fill rate pricing strategy where you charge less than your competitors. This way, you get to increase your occupancy rate and your search ranking simultaneously.

CHAPTER 20
HOW TO GET FIVE-STAR REVIEWS

Getting five-star reviews is another core pillar of the winning formula in the Airbnb business. It is also a key element to qualify as an Airbnb Superhost. Being a Superhost is the ultimate dream for every host because it means more guests and more money. Nonetheless, to reach that level, you need to have at least an average Airbnb rating of 4.8 stars. Getting many five-star reviews is the only way you can have such a rating.

So you see, five-star reviews are not just important because they reveal how much your guests appreciate your services. They also help you attain and maintain the Superhost status while still increasing your search ranking. So as a new Airbnb host, how do you get more five-star reviews?

- Do not make promises you cannot keep!

Some Airbnb hosts try to make a good sales pitch by

describing their Airbnb listing as something it is not. For example, they might say their property has a swimming pool, spa, or gym when it has none of those. Do not do this! Making such promises will only set up your guests for disappointment, which will reduce or even eliminate your chances of getting five-star reviews from them.

So what should you do instead? It is simple—use an honest promotion strategy, so that what your guests see online perfectly matches what they will see on checking in. You could even use the under-promise approach, where you don't let your guests in on everything that your Airbnb offers. Surprising them a little can be a delight.

- Deliver beyond your guests' expectations

If you want a five-star review, then you have to deliver a six-star service to your customers! Usually, you can control the expectations of your guests via your marketing and promotion strategy. So to delight your audience even more, you could deliver something significantly superior to what they expected initially.

An easy way to exceed your guests' expectations is to provide special treats, experiences, or amenities that you know your guests would absolutely love. For example, stocking up on breakfast provisions (like pancake batter, for instance), providing games (like chess), or installing a fully functional coffee bar. Surprises like these not only help you to impress your guests, but also help you stand out from your competitors.

- Address guests' issues promptly

In the typical business world, customers are always right. Similarly, your Airbnb guests would always be right. In fact, in this case, they are more powerful, as they can always leave a review for all future potential guests to see. Thus, if any issues arise with your guests, you must ensure that you resolve those issues as quickly as possible. No matter how flimsy it might sound, treat each of their issues as if it were a HUGE problem!

One thing you must understand is that your potential guests come from different backgrounds. Hence, each guest would have a different standard when it comes to everything from cleaning to house décor. So while one guest might not be bothered about finding hair on the toilet seat, others might demand that the whole bathroom be cleaned again.

- Always send a check-out message

It is always important that you send messages to your Airbnb guests after they check out. This message is supposed to let your guests know that you are all on good terms.

Here is how it works: you could start by thanking the guests for leaving your place in good shape, notwithstanding the actual state they left it in. Then state clearly that you will be leaving a positive review. Finally, you should encourage your guests to provide good feedback directly through the message thread.

Speaking of reviews, how great would it be if you would leave a review for this book on Amazon?

If you've gotten some form of value from this book, or you're just a nice person who likes to support others, please consider leaving a quick review. We personally read all of them and love every time we come across a new one.

I'll even save you the time to find the book, just click on the link below or scan the QR-code on the last page of this book with the camera on your phone.

shorturl.at/ANZQU

Thank you for your support! Now, let's move on to part six.

PART SIX
OPTIMIZING, AUTOMATING, AND SCALING YOUR BUSINESS

CHAPTER 21
AUTOMATING YOUR AIRBNB BUSINESS

As you gradually begin to build and record more profits and occupancy rates in your Airbnb business, your job as a host will tend to become more overwhelming. This development is unsurprising, as we have already established right from the beginning of this book that running an Airbnb business involves an immense investment in money and time. Nonetheless, you still have to efficiently utilize each second of your day to stay ahead of your business operations amid fierce competition.

Now how can you make that possible? Well, this point is where the Airbnb automation strategy comes in to save the day! Airbnb automation is an effective strategy with which you can streamline daily and recurring Airbnb tasks. Some of these tasks include responding to guest messages, adjusting rental pricing, managing the cleanings, and more. Some Airbnb hosts make the mistake of assuming that automation is only designed for large and extremely successful vacation rental companies. However, such an assumption is false. Even if you manage only one Airbnb property, there will be times when things will become very hectic. For instance, if you get to host different families in your apartment four to six times every month, automating the different aspects of your Airbnb in such a situation is critical if you want to satisfy your guests.

Now let's talk about the importance of switching up your Airbnb business with automation functionality to prevent you from having to spend excess time on daily Airbnb operations. Having more time, in turn, increases efficiency and productivity. Ultimately, Airbnb automation accelerates your business growth. In other words, since you are no longer spending time on daily and recurring tasks, you can utilize certain valuable time on your Airbnb business optimization and scaling. Now let's examine some of the critical aspects of your Airbnb business that require automation to enable you to leverage time and enhance your business productivity.

CHAPTER 22
AUTOMATING THE MESSAGING

In the previous section, we identified effective communication and prompt responses as a very important strategy for increasing your search ranks and getting more five-star reviews. These two factors are key elements that Airbnb takes into account in order to grant you the Superhost status, which is the ultimate point of your success on the Airbnb platform.

However, as much as guest communication is beneficial, it is one of the most time-consuming duties of an Airbnb host or property manager. Studies have confirmed that most Airbnb hosts tend to spend 75 percent of their time communicating with their current and potential guests. Spending so much time on just one area of your business is quite unhealthy and risky. Hence, to increase your chances of overall business success, you can consider the following options for automating your message communication:

- Message templates

Usually, the need to communicate with your guests begins right from the very moment your potential guests inquire about the booking, confirm the booking, and complete other major stages of the booking process. So here is how the message templates work: It practically involves creating a list of standard responses that are suitable for both current and potential guests. The list should include your replies to commonly asked questions, booking confirmation messages, welcome messages, etc.

Now, after drafting your messages, you save those replies in a document or spreadsheet so that you will not have to draft new messages every time the need arises. Instead, you could easily copy the messages you have saved.

- Automated messaging systems

Of course, building up an impressive library of message templates for the different stages of Airbnb guest communication saves you from having to draft new messages. Still, you have the task of customizing each of those messages before sending them manually.

However, using automated messaging systems, like Host Tools, might be a better option. With an automated messaging system, you can constantly and effectively communicate with your guests without having to press the send button. How does it work? Firstly, you have to integrate the automated messaging system with your Airbnb account.

Then you create a list of messages to cover every stage of the Airbnb communication flow, right from the point of inquiry till your guests check out.

Once you have completed this task, create message rules for each stage of the Airbnb communication flow. Message rules are a set of criteria that helps the message system determine who to send an automated message to, what specific message to send, when to send it, etc. They also select the events that will trigger the transmission of each set of messages. For example, if you want to communicate with a set of guests who have just confirmed their bookings, all you have to do to trigger and send your message is to select the automatic booking confirmation message.

CHAPTER 23
AUTOMATING THE CLEANING

From what you have learned so far, you have gathered that the cleanliness of your Airbnb property is an important priority for your guests. At the beginning phase of being a typical small-scale Airbnb host, it would have been quite easy for you to handle all the cleaning services of your Airbnb on changeover days. Of course, doing the job yourself saves costs.

However, the expectations of your guests tend to be much higher as you get higher occupancy rates, excellent reviews, and position yourself in a great neighborhood. As such, you have a bigger responsibility to prove yourself deserving of your good rating. A single dirty stain on the toilet seat could create a bad impression and, in turn, cause that particular guest to ruin your hard-earned five-star review record. Essentially, you cannot let such an incident occur, especially at the point when market demand for your Airbnb is constantly increasing.

Therefore, if you have the drive to leverage your time and scale up your Airbnb business, you need to automate your cleaning services by hiring extra hands to help maintain that hotel-like cleanliness that Airbnb guests always appreciate. To automate your Airbnb cleaning, there are two options to choose from:

- Professional cleaning service

Hiring the services of a professional cleaning company is a great automation option. In most cases, when you hire the services of a company, a group of experienced professionals can make your entire property look completely spotless within a few hours.

Since the cleaning is done by a team, the risk of relying on one person is eliminated. You can also be confident that your cleaning appointment will not be canceled if a member of the team is sick or unavailable. Also, professional cleaning companies use the best cleaning equipment.

The major and, perhaps, the only downside to this cleaning automation strategy is the high fee that some of these professional cleaning companies charge. However, this disadvantage can be a good thing for your business in two ways: First, you are assured of the cleanliness of your property, which can generate a great number of five-star reviews for your listing. Secondly, opting for a higher cleaning fee can help attract high-paying guests and not those that are thrifty.

- Hiring an individual cleaning subcontractor

Even if you want to automate your Airbnb business, not everyone can afford the services of a cleaning team. Thus, hiring a subcontractor is a more affordable option to consider. The upside of hiring an individual professional cleaner means that you are charged a smaller fee, and if you have a small or medium-sized Airbnb, the quality of the cleaning service has a higher chance of impressing your guests.

Now how about the downside? It could be a bit risky to rely on a single individual for such an important task as cleaning. Nevertheless, you can easily handle this drawback by having a list of professional cleaning subcontractors from which you can choose to call for help in emergencies.

Extra tips to consider when automating the cleaning

- Always create a suitable incentive structure that aligns your cleaners' interests with yours. For instance, aside from paying your cleaning team the agreed base rate for cleaning during all changeovers, you could also give them a small bonus payment for every five-star cleanliness review.
- Directly forward all the positive and negative guest reviews regarding Airbnb cleanliness to your cleaning team. Doing so encourages them to also have a vested interest in improving the quality of your reviews.
- Have a cleaning checklist with which you can confirm that every area of your Airbnb property is spotless. To

create such a list, you can refer to the section of this book where this was discussed.

CHAPTER 24
AUTOMATING THE PRICING

The rental price of your Airbnb property is often considered to be the first factor influencing your potential guests' booking choice. Even if you have a beautiful house, charging a higher price than the average Airbnb market price can drive away potential guests. Therefore, because of the high impact that pricing has on your booking rate and visibility within Airbnbs' search results, automating this aspect of your Airbnb business is crucial to its growth, especially when you are managing multiple listings.

In the last section of part four of this book, we explicitly analyzed the different types of pricing strategies and tools that you can leverage to automate your pricing process. The entire chapter revealed that trying to price your listing competitively to reflect demand and seasonal variations without using an automation tool is an almost impossible task. This impossibility is rooted in the fact that Airbnb pricing is a constantly fluctuating landscape that changes at an unpredictable rate.

Thus, instead of spending 40-50 percent of your time trying to optimize Airbnb pricing by yourself, you should opt for the more rewarding option of using smart automation pricing tools, like Beyond, PriceLabs, Wheelhouse, etc. To automate your pricing, it is highly recommended that you use the dynamic pricing strategy that was discussed in part four of this book. Perhaps, it would be best if you take a break now to reread part four where we talk about everything related to money in the Airbnb business.

CHAPTER 25
AUTOMATING THE KEY EXCHANGE

A nother time-consuming Airbnb task that you need to automate to optimize and scale up your Airbnb is the key exchange process. The conventional key exchange process usually demands that you directly and physically deliver the keys of your Airbnb space to your guests. Also, you may want to expand the number of Airbnb spaces you rent out as your business grows with more occupancy rates and with more profit. So, in situations where you find yourself hosting remotely from a different city or struggling with a busy schedule, arranging in-person check-ins for your guests can be quite stressful and disorganized.

Therefore, a viable long-term strategy will be necessary for you to automate the key exchange process so that you do not jeopardize your chance of creating a good first impression on your guests. This automated functionality will also help you build a detailed self-check-in system that your guests can use to effortlessly find their way to the Airbnb space.

- Using lockboxes

Lockboxes are storage devices that give Airbnb hosts a secure and easier way to store their rental keys. To prevent unauthorized access, a code designed by the Airbnb host is usually required to open the lockbox.

This self-check-in system is quite durable. All you have to do is inform your guests where to find the lockbox and what the specific code combination to open it is. There are some common lockbox systems with which you can protect your rental keys. Here are some examples:

- Dial Locks

In terms of design, a dial lock look similar to that in a typical gym or high school locker room. To open it, you put in a combination of numbers, then spin the dial.

- Wheel Locks

A wheel lock is a lockbox that has several scrolling wheels numbering 0-9. The number of wheels can vary, though the most common ones consist of four wheels. As such, its code combination is usually a four-digit code. To open a wheel lock, you turn each wheel to select each of the numbers from the code combination.

- Push-Button Lockboxes

When compared to the last two lockboxes described above,

the push-button lockbox is much easier to work with. To get the stored rental keys, your guests need only punch in the correct sequence of the code and the lockbox will open immediately.

- Smart Electronic Locks

This type of lock system is the most advanced and secure option for automating your key exchange process. It eliminates the hassle of having to deal with keys and comes instead in the form of a keypad that is installed on the door.

Using a smart lock also enables you to control who can access your property, even when you are operating remotely. With each booking, you can simply use a phone or computer wherever you are to create a unique code for every guest. It is also perfect for granting access to professionals, such as your plumbers, cleaners, or housekeepers, as you do not have to give them the house keys or your access code.

However, before you install a smart lock on your door, you must consider that a smart lock requires every guest to have a smartphone and enough battery to gain access to your Airbnb property.

- Key exchange service

Apart from using lockboxes, another great option for automating your check-in process is to use key exchange services, like KeyNest and Keycafe.

Here is how this innovative service works: First, you start by integrating your preferred key exchange service account with your Airbnb. Then, you visit any of the key exchange service stores and add a tracking device to your keys, which will be saved in a key storage box.

Once you grant your guests key access, they will receive a notification with the location and access code. They can then pick up keys anytime during the store's opening hours. Since you already have a tracking device on your key, you will be informed of the location of your keys at all times.

CHAPTER 26
AUTOMATING THE ENTIRE PROCESS

As you become more successful in your Airbnb business, there is a good chance that you will start to acquire more rental properties for the business. At that point, the next natural step is for you to automate the entire hosting job by hiring a property manager or a property management company to handle specific tasks and help you manage your properties. In most cases, the responsibility of the Airbnb Property manager is to handle the repetitive day-to-day tasks of your rental properties:

1. They manage your customer services by being in constant communication with both your potential and current guests.

2. When a guest makes an inquiry or requests a booking, they review the guest's ratings and reviews to confirm if the guest is a high-quality guest.

3. They manage maintenance and repairs in your Airbnb

spaces to ensure that everything is working before the arrival of every guest.

4. In cases where you do not reside in the same city as your listings, your property manager could be your physical point of contact with your guests.

Hiring a property manager or property management company involves a great deal of work. Not everyone is qualified for this job and, therefore, you must find a qualified person who is not only capable but also trustworthy. To make things a bit easier for you, here are some evaluation criteria you should consider when choosing a property manager:

- They should be a local of the neighborhood.
- They must have an in-depth knowledge of the Airbnb rental marketing fundamentals.
- They must have a portfolio that implements a diverse set of marketing strategies to boost occupancy rates and profits.
- Their service rates should be affordable and in line with the industry's average rate.

CHAPTER 27
SCALING YOUR AIRBNB BUSINESS

To attain your business and financial goals in the short-term rental market, you have to learn how to scale up your Airbnb business. Scaling up simply involves setting the stage to enable, support, and sustain the growth of your business without necessarily incurring significant costs. In other words, it is a cost-effective way of growing your business in terms of both revenue and booking rates.

One thing to understand is that optimizing and scaling up your Airbnb business depends heavily on your ability to automate the systems and processes of your Airbnb business. Perhaps, you will now understand the reason for using "automation." Automation streamlines the processes of your Airbnb business and ultimately accelerates your business and financial growth.

Most of the stages required for you to scale up your Airbnb business fall under the different automation processes we discussed in the first section. Aside from automating the critical aspects of your Airbnb business—like pricing, cleaning, guest communication, and property management—here are some of the additional steps required to scale up your Airbnb business.

- Build a reliable team.

Building and scaling up your Airbnb business takes more than your expertise as the business's founder. You also need to build a team with complementary skills that are crucial to the overall success of your business. Now, some people may think that it is quite unreasonable to have a team for an Airbnb business of one listing. However, it is not; no matter the number of Airbnb spaces you manage, you cannot single-handedly scale up your business. The consistency and quality of work from your team will have a notable impact on the result of your business.

The essential members of an ideal Airbnb team include the cleaning crew, plumber, electrician, handyman, property manager, and virtual assistants (if you manage multiple listings). Aside from these essential members, you could also have a lawyer, a financial advisor, or an accountant to help with the legal and bookkeeping aspect of your business. Here are some tips you can utilize to build your perfect A-team:

- Set up every team member for success by clearly spelling out your business vision and values; make them understand the importance of these values.
- Build the right culture and environment. This will make the interests of your team members align with yours so that your team will strive to excel.
- Each worker should be a professional in their field. However, you need to specify the kind of results you expect from them. Failure to do so could negatively affect the progress and efficiency of your business.
- Let your team know that you value them by recognizing, rewarding, and motivating them for a job well done.

Once you are sure that each team member fully understands their duty, get out of the way and let them do their best. This step is important because, at the stage of scaling, you are most likely going to become so focused on having a perfect result that you might unconsciously interfere with the activities of your team.

- Establish standardized processes

Flexibility is one of the greatest benefits of running an Airbnb. However, it could hinder the growth of your business in the scale-up stage. If your Airbnb business is going to scale up, you will need to implement standardized and repeatable processes for your daily Airbnb duties. Let's examine an instance of how a standardized Airbnb process works: When a guest requests to book one of your Airbnb listings, you have an automated messaging system that automatically replies and provides them with information about the Airbnb property. Your property manager or virtual assistant, however, does the job of vetting the guests and approving them. Once the booking is approved, your cleaning crew makes the property rental-ready for the guests. On arrival, your smart check-in system is available to grant your guests access to the space. With this example, you can see that there is a kind of standard pattern that guides every process in the Airbnb business.

- Ensure you are ready to grow

Before you begin your journey of scaling up your Airbnb business, you must ensure that you have the necessary resources in terms of operations and processes. The reason for this is that the early stage of your scaling-up process will put your Airbnb business in a very vulnerable position.

Nonetheless, you should understand that scaling up your Airbnb business is a gradual process—it will not happen within weeks. Hence, you must be fully committed to the growth of your Airbnb business.

PART SEVEN
FAQS, ADDITIONAL TIPS AND A LIST OF TOOLS

CHAPTER 28
AIRBNB FAQS

In parts one to six, we successfully covered the core aspects of running a profitable Airbnb business. Nevertheless, we have added this part to ensure that we tie up every loose end as we wrap up. In other words, we will focus on providing you with additional content, tips, resources, and answers to certain questions that we may not have covered in the first six parts of this book.

———

Airbnb FAQs

1. **Q:** What percentage does Airbnb take from hosts?

A: In most cases, Airbnb charges its hosts a three percent service fee. However, the percentage could be higher for hosts in cities with Super Strict Cancellation policies or those in the Airbnb Plus program.

2. **Q:** Should I only use Airbnb for my short-term rental?

A: Airbnb is not the only company operating in the short-term rental market. Its major competitors include Vrbo, Flipkey, HomeAway, House Trip, etc.

3. **Q:** What do I do when a guest asks to book offline?

A: Your best option is to politely decline the guest's request to book their stay offline. However, you must be careful not to insinuate in any way that the guest is untrustworthy. Instead, you could use taxes or your desire to get a Superhost status as an excuse for not granting their requests.

4. **Q:** What do I do if a guest steals from my property?

A: The first thing to do is confirm if the item(s) was actually stolen. Once you have evidence that the guest stole some of your belongings, make a list of the stolen items and immediately contact Airbnb. Keep in mind that your claim will be considered invalid if it is not submitted within 14 days after your guest checks out.

5. **Q:** What are the requirements to become a Superhost?

A: Airbnb stipulates four basic criteria that hosts must satisfy to become Superhost. Firstly, you must host a minimum of ten stays in a year. Secondly, you must maintain at least a 90 percent fast response rate to both your current and potential guests. Thirdly, five-star reviews must make up at least 80 percent of your overall reviews. Finally, you must be a host who rarely cancels confirmed reservations.

6. **Q**: What are the best locks to use for my Airbnb space?

A: Though smart locks are quite pricey, they are the best locks for securing your Airbnb space. They also make it easier for you to control who gains entry into your property.

7. **Q**: Do I really need an LLC for my Airbnb business?

A: Running an Airbnb business could involve a high amount of risk, especially when you begin to scale up. Thus, instead of registering your Airbnb space in your own name, it is better to form an LLC so that you can protect your personal assets with limited liability protection. It also enables you to enjoy more tax options while building your business's credibility.

8. **Q:** Why am I getting more notes from landlords?

A: It could be that you are doing things the wrong way. One incorrect way to approach a landlord for a rental arbitrage is to try to pitch your sales through a phone call, text, or email. Every attempt you make has to be in person. Before anything, you have to build a trusting relationship with that landlord. A series of solid and meaningful conversations about their families, jobs, or hobbies could do the trick. Simply doing these actions beforehand makes it easier for you to get them to listen to your pitch.

9. **Q:** Should I get extra insurance?

A: Yes, it is important that you do not only rely on the Airbnb Host Guarantee of $1 million, which only covers your major losses but not damages caused by wear and tear. Thus, whether you are a renter or a homeowner, you need to purchase extra business insurance for double coverage.

CHAPTER 29
ADDITIONAL TIPS

To top it off, we have provided additional tips for those who are are willing to go the extra mile and take their Airbnb business to the next level.

———

Airbnb Experiences

In 2016, Airbnb launched a new platform called Airbnb Experiences. The goal of the program was to offer Airbnb guests and travelers the chance to discover the unique essence of local places and enjoy personalized experiences with local experts. The platform was further diversified with an online version in April 2020. Airbnb Online Experiences enable guests across different cities of the world to enjoy classes, performances, shows, and other local experiences from the comfort of their homes.

Now, you must understand that Airbnb Experiences are a separate service on Airbnb from Airbnb Property Hosting. As a host who wants to offer experiences to Airbnb guests, you do not have to rent out a property to offer an experience.

Nevertheless, Airbnb rental hosts can also join the Airbnb Experiences program to increase their income. Since you already have the license to run your Airbnb business in your city, you can easily promote your Airbnb business to your property rental guests by informing them that you offer Airbnb Experiences, which you can sell as an upgrade to your property listing.

What qualities must you have to qualify for hosting Airbnb Experiences?

1. You must have immense knowledge in the experience you want to offer.

2. You must be ready to provide an interactive atmosphere in all cases.

3. The experience should be a unique niche on its own. It has to be an activity that is not easily available to your potential guest.

What experiences can you offer on Airbnb?

As of the time of writing this book, there are over 40,000 activities in more than 1,000 cities around the world that guests can book on the Airbnb Experiences platform. Keep in mind that you cannot offer general tours or sight-seeing guides as Airbnb Experiences. Here are some categories of experiences you can choose to offer:

- Food and drinks—wine or pasta tastings, a masterclass in coffee-making, or a cooking tutorial on how to make classic street food.
- Nature—hiking tours on famous mountains and visits to forests and shrines.
- Health and wellness—meditation and yoga classes.
- Arts and entertainment—musical shows, operas, local concerts, theatre performances, etc.
- History—walking tours in historical places across the world.

How do you register for Airbnb experiences?

Having created the exact experience you want to offer, upload images and descriptions regarding the local experience. However, you cannot offer the experience to guests until you have first been approved by Airbnb. Thus, you must formally apply to join the Airbnb Experiences Program.

The Airbnb team reviews your application by analyzing the quality and standards of your experience. Generally, the waiting period takes less than two weeks. Once the Airbnb team contacts you to inform you that your application has been approved, you can begin hosting online or physically.

Pros

- The Airbnb Experiences program offers you a convenient and exhilarating chance to earn money while doing what you love and are passionate about.
- As a property host, hosting an experience can help increase your booking rate and Airbnb income.
- While you can only host a few guests at a time in your Airbnb space, Airbnb Experiences hosts can accommodate an entire group of guests at once.

Cons

- Airbnb charges hosts in the Airbnb Experiences program twenty percent of the final price, which is higher than the regular three percent Airbnb service fee.
- If you decide to host a rental property and an experience together, you will be charged separately for both offerings by Airbnb.

Making Your Airbnb "Event-Ready"

Apart from offering experiences, designing your Airbnb property to be "event ready" is another effective strategy that can serve as a lucrative revenue stream. This idea is quite useful, especially during the low season when there are fewer bookings. Now, by events, we mean professional or semi-professional occasions with commercial benefits. Depending on the size of your space, these events could be house parties, weddings, intimate meetings, retreats, filming, or TV commercials.

How do you Register your Airbnb as an Event Venue?

In order to get proper documentation to host events in your Airbnb, a home inspection may be required by your local government. After your place has been approved, you might also need to acquire additional permits. For example, your guests might want to serve alcohol during certain events. You may need a permit to host such events. Also, renting out your Airbnb space for events may incur additional tax payments, and you may need to get extra insurance. How do you make your Airbnb property convenient enough for guests attending the events?

Seating: The living rooms in a typical Airbnb space, including luxurious Airbnb spaces, do not have enough seating for 50-100 people. Depending on the exact type of event that will be held in your Airbnb space, you must ensure that you rent enough chairs, tables, and perhaps bean bags (if it is a casual hangout) to accommodate every guest.

Restrooms: Just like your Airbnb living rooms, your toilets and bathrooms might also be ill-equipped to handle the needs of the number of guests you are expecting. To ensure your guests don't have to wait in line to use the restrooms, you could consider making a few porta-potties available during the event. Taking such an action could even save your septic system from being overused.

AV requirements: In certain cases, the guests are responsible for providing the necessary equipment, like microphones, sound systems, projectors, etc. Despite whose responsibility it is to provide the audio and visual equipment, as the Airbnb host, you must confirm and inform your guests ahead of time about the noise policy for your neighborhood.

Dishes: Turning your Airbnb space into an event venue may also mean that you have to hire a catering company to provide refreshments for the events. However, you could have a different arrangement where your guests would be the ones responsible for the catering during the events.

Parking: The issue of parking is another important factor to consider when turning your Airbnb into an event venue. Your limited parking space could be a problem; as such, you may have to improvise or find extra space for your guests to park their vehicles. In cases where some of your guests want to stay overnight, you would have to install a surveillance system or hire a security guard to provide adequate security for their vehicles.

- Incorporating an electronic guide

In previous chapters, we emphasized the importance of providing your guests with an explicit house manual that answers all their likely questions about operations, basic amenities, facilities, etc. Having a house manual box in your Airbnb listing is most appropriate at the beginning of your Airbnb business. However, as your occupancy rate and profits increase, using a single text box may not be enough to take you to the next level.

So, you need to automate this aspect of your Airbnb business by opting for a digital option. Integrating a digital guide into your Airbnb space enables your guests to conveniently use and read the instructions with their smartphones or operating devices. They also do not have to deal with the hassle of carrying papers around.

As an Airbnb host, opting for a digital Airbnb guide makes it easier for you to implement changes and updates into your listing wherever you are. This easiness comes without your having to print pages or swap an in-house guidebook or manual.

Reviewing Your Airbnb Guests

Writing the perfect guest review, whether it is a positive review or a negative one, can be quite problematic. Sometimes, you just don't have anything to say about a guest. It could also be that you have important and positive things to say about your guest, yet you cannot seem to find the right words to precisely express your thoughts. Also, if the review is a negative one, you might find it hard to warn other hosts about this guest without sounding vindictive. Well, here are a few tips you can use to write the perfect positive or negative Airbnb guest review.

Positive reviews

- Keep them simple, straightforward, and honest. For example, you could write a positive review by simply telling your guests that they are welcome to visit you again.

- You could make them personal. For instance, you could mention how you shared a special moment with your guests.
- Emphasizing the ease of communication between you and your guests can make a great review.
- Finally, acknowledge what you like about your guests or the good things that a guest did that made them stand out.

Negative reviews

- In writing negative reviews, you have to be more specific. If you are giving your guests a one-star review, succinctly explain your reason for doing so.
- Don't try to sugarcoat the wrongdoings of your guests. For example, saying, "She was a good guest but she disobeyed my house rules by bringing in a pet." In this case, sticking to the second part of your statement would be more preferable.
- Acknowledge that you would not want to host the guest again.
- Above all, resist the urge to be vindictive; instead, remain cool, calm, and collected.

Engaging Better with Your Airbnb Guests

Here are some tips from seasoned hosts and property managers on how you can build better host-guest relationships:

- A positive host-guest relationship begins with a friendly intro. So, sometimes you could go out of your way to make your guests feel more welcome with small gestures like adding a handwritten welcome note or giving them gift baskets.
- Approach your guests with empathy and show them that you trust them to treat your space as their own home. Not creating a long list of what not to do in the house manual could be helpful here.
- Consistent communication is crucial to a great host-guest engagement. As such, you should make it mandatory to keep in touch with your guests before, during, and after each stay.
- Ensure that you respect their personal boundaries. As a host, you must be sensitive enough to distinguish when a guest wants to have conversations with you and when they want their privacy.
- Personalize your hospitality by asking questions that will help you tailor your recommendation to your guests' needs. For example, you could ask beforehand if your guests have any dietary restrictions so you can recommend the best restaurants to them.
- Be available and responsive when necessary, especially when there is an issue with or complaint from your guests.

How to Contact Airbnb

As a host, there are many different ways to contact Airbnb. You could contact the company either by calling their phone numbers, sending an email, or using the live chat feature on the Airbnb website. You could also send them a message via their social media platforms. Nonetheless, calling the Airbnb customer service line directly on the phone is one of the most effective ways to get a quick response to your complaints or requests. It is more likely to get your calls answered quickly because the phone lines are open twenty-four hours a day, seven days a week.

Tools Mentioned in the Book

Market Research:

- AirDNA's Market Minder
- AirDNA's Investment Explorer
- AirDNA's Rentalizer
- AirDNA's Mashvisor

Price Automation:

- PriceLabs
- Beyond
- Wheelhouse

Automated messaging systems:

- Host Tools

CONCLUSION

When we first set out to be Airbnb hosts, we had no experience nor an atom of the knowledge you must have gotten from reading this book. Back then, we were more concerned about renting our room simply to make money on the side. Initially, we struggled a lot because most of the aspects covered in this book were things we had to learn on the job. Fortunately for you, you now have all it takes to be a great host from your first day and ultimately grow to become a Superhost. Now, let's take a walk down the memory lane of this knowledge-filled adventure, shall we?

At the very start, we introduced you to the overall fundamentals of what it is like to run an Airbnb business. Then, we introduced you properly to the processes involved in the planning stage of an Airbnb business, from the point of choosing the perfect business structure for your Airbnb to that of conducting adequate Airbnb market research. In the same way that soldiers cannot win wars without their weapons, as an Airbnb host, you also cannot succeed in the Airbnb game without first having adequate knowledge about the Airbnb market and the elements within it.

Having completed the paperwork side, the book provided you with explicit information on the practical process of running an Airbnb business. Some of these practical processes include setting up different parts of your Airbnb space, installing essential amenities in each of these spaces, deep cleaning your Airbnb space in between guest visits, creating an explicit house manual and a list of house rules, and more.

In order to ensure that you have adequate knowledge of the financial side of the game, we discussed everything related to money in the Airbnb market. We analyzed the exact methods to make money in the short-term rental market, the different expenses you will most likely incur, and, most importantly, the best Airbnb pricing strategies. Additionally, we revealed the elements that make up the Airbnb winning formula and how you can incorporate them to grow your occupancy rate and increase your revenue.

With everything we discussed in this book, the fact remains that your Airbnb journey will not be a walk in the park. Nonetheless, this book has identified the pitfalls you are likely to encounter at every stage of building your Airbnb business. With this knowledge, you have a much better chance to avoid those mistakes and more easily overcome those challenges.

Like we said in the introduction of this book, everyone deserves to have a job with which they can live their best lives while helping other people enjoy the best travel and hospitality experience. We have fulfilled our promise by providing you with all the necessary knowledge, resources, and tools. It is now time for you to take a big step to start, grow, and maintain a profitable and successful Airbnb business!

RESOURCES

Badia, E. (2019). THJ 33: How to Build and Keep a Team for your Airbnb. Retrieved from file:///storage/emulated/0/Down load/THJ%2033_%20How%20to%20Build%20and%20-Keep%20a%20Team%20for%20your%20Airbnb.mhtml

Baker, H. (2019). 8 Characteristics of Top Property Managers. Retrieved from https://www.mashvisor.com/blog/character istics-top-property-managers/amp/

Duckworth, I. (2019). 11 Helpful Examples of Airbnb House Rules. Retrieved from https://bnbduck.com/11-helpful-examples-of-airbnb-house-rules/

Esajian, JD. (2021). Investing In Airbnb Rentals for Beginners. Retrieved from https://www.fortunebuilders.com/airbnb-rentals/

Evans, A. (2019). 34 Amenities for Your Airbnb That Go The Extra Mile & That Your Guests Will Love. Retrieved from https://medium.com/@allanevans_1809/34-amenities-for-your-airbnb-that-go-the-extra-mile-that-your-guests-will-love-9265039d06a2

Hosty. (2018). "What is the Airbnb Experience and Its Benefits? Retrieved from https://www.hostyapp.com/airbnb-experience/

iGMS, (2020). Airbnb House Rules: Examples and a Free Template for Hosts. Retrieved from https://www.igms.com/airbnb-house-rules/

iGMS, (2020). Airbnb Automation: 7 Ways to Put Your Business on Autopilot. Retrieved from https://www.igms.com/automate-airbnb/

iGMS, (2020). Airbnb Lockbox: How to Provide Self-Check-In to Your Guests. Retrieved from https://www.igms.com/airbnb-lockbox/

iGMS, (2019). How to Write Airbnb Guest Reviews [Examples Included]. Retrieved from https://www.igms.com/getting-airbnb-guest-reviews-101/

Global Guessing. (2019) How to Automate Your Airbnb Business And Scale To a Multi-Million Dollar Business? Retrieved from http://globalguesting.com/2019/06/22/how-to-automate-your-airbnb-business-and-scale-to-a-multi-million-dollar-business/

GuestReady, (2017). How to Write an Awesome Description

for your Airbnb Listing. Retrieved from https://www. guestready.com/blog/airbnb-description-tips/

Jasper. (2019). The Ultimate Guide to Scaling Your Airbnb Business Without Owning Property. Retrieved from https:// getpaidforyourpad.com/blog/scaling-your-airbnb-business-guide/

Kamel, M. (2019). What You Should Know About Hosting an Experience On Airbnb. Retrieved from https://pro.regiondo. com/airbnb-experiences-host/

Karani, A. (2019). Buying Property For Airbnb Is Still A Smart Move! Here's why. Retrieved from https://www.mashvisor. com/blog/buying-property-wfor-airbnb-smart-move/ [URL inactive]

Kevin, P. (2021). Making Money with Airbnb in 2021: Why I Rent Out Our Guest Room. Retrieved from https://financialpanther.com/making-money-airbnb-rent-guest-room/

Knapp, S. (2018). Airbnb Warning Signs How to Avoid Bad Listings. Retrieved from https://medium.com/steph-knapp/airbnb-warning-signs-how-to-avoid-bad-listings-751ff97d11b2

Lake, R. (2021). Does Your Homeowner's Insurance Cover Airbnb? Retrieved from https://www.investopedia.com/articles/insurance/120816/does-your-homeowners-insurance-cover-airbnb.asp

Learnabnb. (2015). 5 Tips to Earning a 5-Star Review on Airbnb. Retrieved from https://learnbnb.com/earning-a-5-star-review-on-airbnb/

Maina, M. (2020). How to Scale Up Your Airbnb Business. Retrieved from https://www.beverlyhillsmagazine.com/how-to-scale-up-your-airbnb-business/

Matt, M. (2018). 7 TIPS TO BOOK AIRBNBS FOR PARTIES. Retrieved from https://mojomatt.me/tips-book-airbnb-parties/

Papineau, N. (2017). How to Boost your Income by Becoming an Airbnb Co-Host? Retrieved from https://www.airbnbsecrets.com/airbnb-co-host/

Parkinson, R. (2019). 21 Common Mistakes Airbnb Hosts Make. Retrieved from https://www.satisfiedsleepers.com/21-common-mistakes-airbnb-hosts-make/

Philip, H. (2021). Dynamic Pricing: PriceLabs VS Wheelhouse VS Beyond. Retrieved from https://www.smoobu.com/en/blog/dynamic-smart-pricing-pricelabs-vs-wheelhouse-vs-beyond-pricing/

Pristine Professional Cleaning. (2019). Our Step by Step Airbnb Cleaning Checklist. Retrieved from https://pristinecleaning.com.au/our-step-by-step-airbnb-cleaning-checklist/

Rooney, D. (2020). What to Know Before Using Airbnb for Your Next Event Space. Retrieved from https://www.eventbrite.com/blog/airbnb-event-space/

Rusteen, D. (2017). Use Your Phone to Take Better Airbnb Photos. Retrieved from https://optimizemybnb.com/better-airbnb-photos/

Salter, P. (2015). The Six Steps to Scaling a Business. Retrieved from https://www.google.com/amp/s/www.forbes.com/sites/philipsalter/2016/05/02/the-six-steps-to-scaling-a-business/amp/

Schuster, P. (2015). Airbnb cleaning: 5 Biggest Mistakes You Should Always Avoid. Retrieved from https://blog.made comfy.com.au/5-common-airbnb-cleaning-issues-that-hurt-your-property-performance.

Stone Field, J. (2020). What to Know Before Renting Out Your Home on Airbnb. Retrieved from https://www.forbes.com/sites/nextavenue/2020/02/04/what-to-know-before-renting-out-your-home-on-airbnb/?sh=2a3d69a35d55.

The Hospitable Team. (2020). Airbnb House Rules: Actionable Tips and Templates. Retrieved from https://hospitable.com/airbnb-house-rules/

Touch Stay, (2019). The Airbnb Guidebook | 4 Alternative Solutions Retrieved from https://touchstay.com/airbnb-guidebook/.

Tom, (2020). Airbnb Host Fees: How Much Is Airbnb Charging You? An Up-To-Date Guide. Retrieved from https://hosttools.com/blog/airbnb-rentals/airbnb-host-fees/

Uprety, M. (2020). Top 10 Mistakes Airbnb Hosts Make. Retrieved from https://www.lodgify.com/blog/airbnb-hosts-mistakes/

Weaver, T. (2020). 11 Airbnb Hosting Mistakes to Avoid (Key Tips from a Pro). Retrieved from https://financialwolves.com/airbnb-hosting-tips/

Wong, A. (2020). Catchy Airbnb Title Examples (To Stand Out and Get Bookings). Retrieved from https://alexwongcopywriting.com/catchy-airbnb-title-examples/

Zuo, S. (2019). How to Make More Money by Becoming an Airbnb Co-Host. Retrieved from https://www.passiveairbnb.com/make-money-becoming-airbnb-co-host/

Zuo, S. (2019). How much will this Airbnb Business Cost Me to Start? Retrieved from https://www.passiveairbnb.com/how-much-will-this-airbnb-business-cost-me-to-start/

To leave a review, you can:

- Scan the QR-code below with the camera on your phone to go directly to the review page.
- Or type in the Shorturl link below the QR-code in your internet browser.

shorturl.at/ANZQU

We appreciate your support!

Made in the USA
Columbia, SC
20 November 2022

71619417R00117